SACRED SITES

SEARCHING FOR BOOK OF MORMON LANDS

JOSEPH L. ALLEN, PhD

Covenant Communications, Inc.

Cover image, *Izapa, Stela 5,* © Cliff Dunstan.

Cover design copyrighted 2003 by Covenant Communications, Inc.

Published by Covenant Communications, Inc.
American Fork, Utah

Copyright © 2003 by Joseph L. Allen

All rights reserved. No part of this book may be reproduced in any format or in any medium without the written permission of the publisher, Covenant Communications, Inc., P.O. Box 416, American Fork, UT 84003. The views expressed herein are the responsibility of the author and do not necessarily represent the position of Covenant Communications, Inc.

Printed in China
First Printing: November 2003

10 09 08 07 06 05 04   10 9 8 7 6 5 4 3

ISBN 1-59156-272-4

TABLE OF CONTENTS

INTRODUCTION
    Sacred Geography 1

CHAPTER ONE
    Lehi's Landing Site 17

CHAPTER TWO
    Up to Nephi 27

CHAPTER THREE
    Down to Zarahemla 43

CHAPTER FOUR
    The East Wilderness 55

CHAPTER FIVE
    The Land of Bountiful 63

CHAPTER SIX
    The Land of Desolation 71

CHAPTER SEVEN
    Monte Albán 83

CHAPTER EIGHT
    Teotihuacan 89

CHAPTER NINE
    Dark and Loathsome 95

CHAPTER TEN
    Pure and Delightsome 101

SOMEWHERE IN THE VAST WILDERNESS, THERE LIES—

WHERE SILENCE REIGNS SUPREME, VOICES STILLED—

A LAND BEFORE CALLED ZARAHEMLA.

SMOTHERED UNDER ROOTS OF ANCIENT TREES,

SCARRING THE SURFACE OF PLAINS AND VALLEYS

(VERNON W. LARSEN, OUT OF THE DUST,
PROMISED LAND PUBLICATIONS, 1980, 7)

INTRODUCTION
SACRED GEOGRAPHY

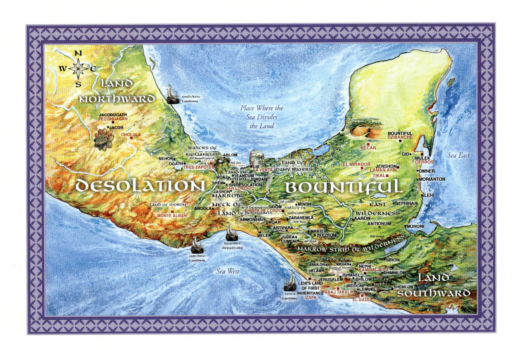

a choice land

Enough information is available from both the Jaredite record and the Nephite record to determine that the people of the Book of Mormon were part of a high civilization. This means that they had a written language, they had a centralized government, they had a religious hierarchy, and they had controlled trade activity. Inasmuch as the area called Mesoamerica is the only place in all of the Americas that meets these requirements, we are obligated to examine meticulously that particular area for potential evidence of Book of Mormon sites.

Mesoamerica encompasses South and Southeastern Mexico, Guatemala, El Salvador, Honduras, Belize, and parts of Costa Rica and Nicaragua. In addition to its geographical meaning, the term "Mesoamerica" also refers to that time period prior to the Conquest of Mexico and the many great civilizations that flourished in Middle America during the pre-Columbian periods. Mesoamerican civilizations date from approximately 2800 B.C. to A.D. 1500.

History reports that several of these Mesoamerican civilizations existed during the Book of Mormon period. They include the lowland and highland Maya, the Olmec culture along the Gulf Coast of Mexico,

Above: Mesoamerica includes south and southeastern Mexico, Guatemala, Belize, El Salvador, and Honduras and relates to the pre-Columbian time period.

Opposite: The delicate magenta flower from Antigua, Guatemala, reflects the beauty of the land, its people, its culture and its history.

Above: This large, outdoor relief map of Guatemala is located in Guatemala City. The view is from the south-eastern side of Mexico looking towards Belize and the highlands of Guatemala. The Petén rain forest, referred to as the southern Maya lowlands, is in the foreground. From a Book of Mormon perspective, the land of Nephi was south in the mountains and the Land of Zarahemla was north in the lowlands.

the Zapotec culture core in the Valley of Oaxaca, and the Teotihuacan culture core in the Valley of Mexico. The Mexican states of Mexico, Puebla, Morelos, Guerrero, Michoacan, Hidalgo, Tlaxcala, Veracruz, Oaxaca, Tabasco, Chiapas, Campeche, Yucatan, and Quintana Roo are all part of Mesoamerica. Oaxaca and Chiapas have the highest native populations of the Republic of Mexico, and the Yucatan is still home to many Mayan communities.

A sizeable part of Mesoamerica is made up from the twenty-two departments (states) of Guatemala, a country that has become very significant to Book of Mormon history. For this reason it is also important to note that, historically, both the small country of Belize and the Mexican state of Chiapas were also a part of Guatemala. Guatemala has approximately ten million inhabitants, with one-half of that number considered native to Guatemala. Yet Guatemala's ten million is a far cry from Mexico's nearly 100 million inhabitants. The population of Mexico far outnumbers any other country that now forms ancient Mesoamerica, and the native population of Mesoamerica itself outnumbers the native population of the United States and Canada 100 to one.

Mesoamerica is almost completely surrounded by water. The topography is variable, consisting of dense jungles, high mountain regions, and tropical lowlands. The highest mountain peak is Mount Orizaba, stretching 18,400 feet into the air. In contrast, the area in and around Villahermosa, Tabasco, measures several feet below sea level. Many of the natives live along the coast and in the mountains.

The climate of Mesoamerica is also variable. Mexico City, with an elevation of 7,400 feet, maintains an average of 72 degrees Fahrenheit year round. Guatemala City, at 4,900 feet elevation, is also ideal year round. The jungle lowlands, however, are extremely hot and humid—drenched by Mesoamerica's rainy season, which lasts from May to October.[2]

THE REGIONS ROUND ABOUT

For those students of the Book of Mormon who find it difficult to understand the Isaiah chapters that Nephi included—you are not alone. Even Nephi's immediate audience struggled, for he admitted that the words "were hard for many of [his] people to understand" (2 Ne. 25:1). But his confession did not constitute an apology, for he knew that these prophetic passages would point his people to Christ. And yet along with his acknowledgment came an explanation for the Nephites' difficulty—Nephi realized that his "people of the promised land" were far removed from Jerusalem and did not understand the Jews' manner of prophesying. In other words, not only were the Nephites unschooled in the Jews' tra-

ditions, but they also had never lived in their *land*. Nephi wrote, "I, of myself, have dwelt at Jerusalem, wherefore I know concerning the regions round about" (2 Ne. 25:1-7).

Nephi taught that, among other factors such as being filled with the spirit of prophecy, one of the essential keys to understanding scripture is to understand "the regions round about." Therefore, if geography helps us to understand the Isaiah chapters, then let us apply the same principle to the entire Book of Mormon. The day has passed where we can say we don't have enough evidence of Book of Mormon geography or that it is not important. Both statements lack substance. The science of archaeology and the spirit of prophecy promised by President Ezra Taft Benson have combined, allowing us to (1) more fully understand the geography and culture of the Book of Mormon, and (2) understand the spiritual message behind the geographical and cultural symbols.

If one of the major keys to understanding the Book of Mormon lies in our knowledge of its history, culture, and geography, then learning more about each of these elements is invaluable. And that is the primary purpose of this book—to bring to life the historical and geographical elements of the Book of Mormon. It will also show how, in most instances, these details can lead us to Christ, which is the ultimate purpose of the Book of Mormon. For this reason, it is sacred geography.

Below: The ancient Maya ruins of Palenque, Chiapas, Mexico, is representative of the massive tombs and buildings that were built throughout Mesoamerica during the Classic period from A.D. 250 to 900. The pyramid in the center of the photo was uncovered in 1952 by Alberto Ruz. Originally called the Temple of Inscriptions, it is now called the Tomb of Pacal Na who died in A.D. 684.

Right: A hieroglyph identifiable on the Pyramid of the Inscriptions (Tomb of Pacal Na) has been interpreted as "and then it came to pass," a phrase that is common in the Book of Mormon. A phonetic written language surfaced in the middle of the 2nd century B.C. in Mesoamerica—the same time that the Nephite written language began to circulate among the Lamanites (Mosiah 24:2-6).

4 SACRED SITES

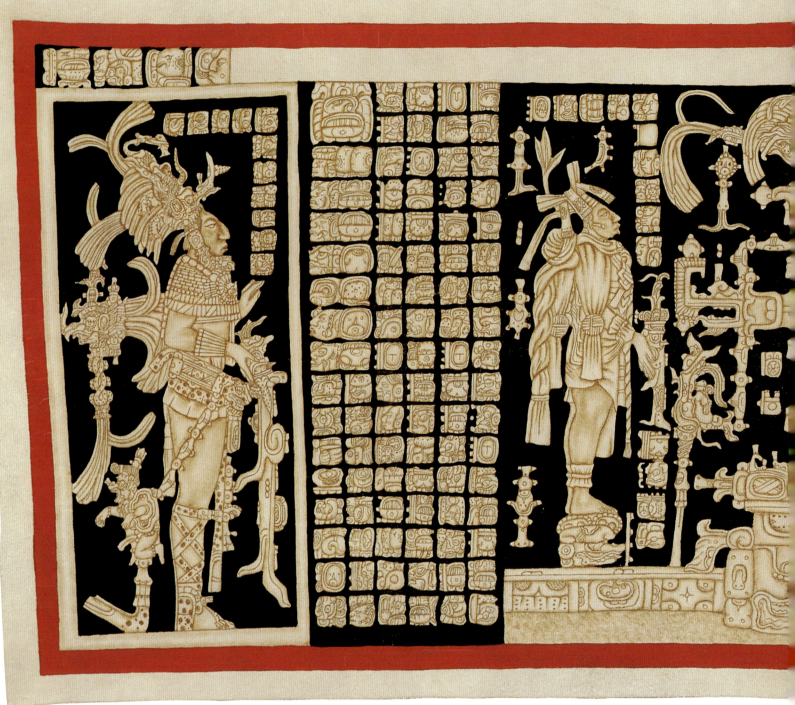

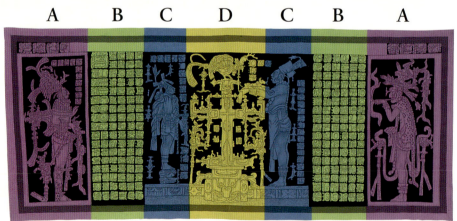

A B C D C B A

SACRED GEOGRAPHY 5

The Temple of the Cross at Palenque (located in the foreground in the photo on page 3) manifests a Hebrew writing style called "chiasmus" and is written in the same format as the entire book of first Nephi. Dates to A.D. 700. The Quetzal bird is on the center top panel and the "coatl" serpent, or earth monster motif, is on the bottom part of the center panel. Quetzal-Coatl portrayed the same imagery to the Classic Maya as Christ hanging on a cross portrayed to the seventh-century Catholic Church.

Inverted Hebrew parallelism or chiasmus is manifested on the Temple of the Cross in a typical A-B-C-D-C-B-A format. Notice that the center panel of the 7th century A.D. mural is associated with Quetzalcoatl, similar to the way the central portion of 1 Nephi relates to Christ. The two panels labeled "C" show the father Pacal Na on the left and his son Chan Balam on the right, much in the same way that Lehi and Nephi relate to each other in the analysis of the Tree of Life. The two panels labeled "A" are important ancestral figures in the same way that Lehi occupies the first position in first Nephi and Isaiah is quoted in the final chapters. The "B" panels also show historical movements in both 1 Nephi and the Temple of the Cross. That the Classic Maya would continue this style of writing after the close of the Book of Mormon is quite remarkable.

6 SACRED SITES

Above Top: Three icons carved from basalt stone were discovered at the Olmec site of La Venta along the Gulf of Mexico. Representative of Olmec art from 1200–300 B.C.

Above: Monument 22 at the La Venta park in Villahermosa suggests that the first settlers of Mesoamerica came across the ocean as indicated by a man fending off a sea monster (see Ether 6:10).

Right: Engraved Olmec monument from La Venta, Tabasco. Dates to the Jaredite time period, 1200–300 B.C.

Opposite: Maya dignitaries from the Chiapas mountains near Ocosingo, Chiapas, Mexico, dressed in their native costumes. The state of Chiapas hosts the highest percentage ratio of the native population of Mexico.

SACRED GEOGRAPHY

A STANDARDIZED CRITERIA

The Book of Mormon is an abridgement of the record of the Nephites and the Lamanites, as well as an abridgement taken from the book of Ether concerning the Jaredites. It is a real history. It speaks of real people. The events recorded within its pages actually happened somewhere. While its purpose is neither to present a chronological history of the Nephites nor to set forth a precise geographical picture of where they lived, both history and geography are recorded within its pages.

Any legitimate study of Book of Mormon geography must adhere to at least four criteria, and it is this adherence that enables us to accurately determine if a proposed site is legitimate. Most current literature supports the idea that the heartland of Book of Mormon culture takes place in the area called Mesoamerica. Justification for such is based on the following elements:

LANGUAGE

The majority of the Book of Mormon was written during 600 B.C. to A.D. 421. The only place where a written, phonetic language has been discovered that dates back to this one-thousand-year period and which encompasses high civilizations, is in the areas located on both sides of the Isthmus of Tehuantepec, in Mesoamerica.

Archaeology

The Book of Mormon speaks of many cities built over a long period of time. The Jaredite civilization dates from about 2800 to 300 B.C., the Lamanite-Nephite and the Mulekite-Nephite histories from 600 B.C. to A.D. 400, with the Lamanite culture continuing well beyond A.D. 400. Again, it is the only place in the Americas where culture and population centers meet the requirement of a high civilization in Mesoamerica.

History

Mesoamerica holds many cultural traditions in common, including the arrival of the first settlers from the great tower, and accounts of the white god, Quetzalcoatl. These oral and written traditions, along with the modern-day cultural patterns emerging from Mesoamerica, mirror those found in the Book of Mormon.

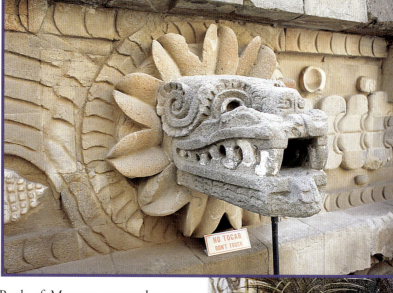

Geography

The geography found in the Book of Mormon is adequate and distinct. The Mesoamerican map matches in striking detail the layout reported in the Book of Mormon. Book of Mormon geography must include not only a study of mountains, lands, waters, trade routes, etc., but also must include directions, distances, and cultural and linguistic parallels.[1]

A Choice Seer

Two men—one Joseph Smith, Jr., and the other John Lloyd Stephens—were both born in the year 1805. While there is no evidence that the two ever met, their paths seemed to cross indirectly. Both were historically significant, Joseph Smith known as "the great American prophet," and John Stephens as the father of Mesoamerican archaeology. Ironically, Stephens studied under the very professor who essayed to discredit Joseph Smith's work, Professor Charles Anthon. He appears to be the "learned man" to whom Martin Harris took a brief excerpt of the translated work, often referred to as the Anthon manuscript of the Book of Mormon, and who reportedly declared that he could "not read a sealed book" (see 2 Ne. 27:16–17).

Several other similarities exist between these two men. For example, a portion of Stephens's travels appears to follow the same trail where a number of migrations outlined in the Book of Mormon occurred. Joseph Smith was assisted in his work of bringing forth the Book of Mormon by, among others, a scribe named Oliver Cowdery. John Stephens was assisted in his work by an artist named Frederick Catherwood. Joseph Smith, Jr. was that "choice seer" who translated the Book of Mormon.

SACRED GEOGRAPHY   9

The religious tradition surrounding the serpent motif is both a Book of Mormon and a Mesoamerica theme. Coatl is a Nahuatl (Aztec) name, whereas Can is a Maya name, both meaning serpent. The feathered-serpent god is the most prominent god of all Mesoamerican cultures. Left inset: Teotihuacan serpent with feathered collar motif from the temple of Quetzalcoatl near Mexico City. Dates to A.D. 300. Center: Painting by Frederick Catherwood. Maya/Toltec serpent motif from the temple of Kukulcan at Chichen Itza. Dates to A.D. 1200. Right inset: Olmec serpent motif dating to 300 B.C. from La Venta, Tabasco.

10 SACRED SITES

Mesoamerica is a land of beauty and contrasts. In excess of thirty-five volcanic mountains grace the landscape of the country of Guatemala. Guatemala is about one-third the size of the state of Utah.

Left top: A boat ride down the Grijalva River (proposed Sidon) through the majestic Sumidero Canyon affords an abundant view of wildlife, including monkeys, crocodiles, vultures, and the long-necked, copper-colored cranes shown here.

Left second from top: Flowers dot the landscape of Lehi's promised land.

Left third from top: Towering volcanoes serve as boundaries and historic reminders. Shown here is the Tacana volcanic mountain that divides Mexico and Guatemala.

Above: The ruins of Abaj Takalik located along the Pacific coast of Guatemala manifest both Olmec and Maya architecture, indicating that remnants of the Jaredites were living in the area where Lehi landed shortly after 600 B.C. The Mayans may have evolved into the Lamanite and Nephite cultures after 570 B.C.

Above: This map of Mesoamerica outlines the locations of the major cultures that existed during the time period of the Book of Mormon. Olmec: 2500 B.C.—300 B.C.; Zapotec 500 B.C.—700 A.D.; Teotihuacan 300 B.C.—700 A.D.; Maya 800 B.C.—1500 A.D.

SACRED GEOGRAPHY 11

John Lloyd Stephens wrote about his travels and paved the way for further study in Mesoamerican archaeology. The Book of Mormon and the books written by Stephens are both still in circulation today. It is interesting that the lives of these two men paralleled each other so closely, so much so that it appears that they both wrote about the same ancient people. One wrote its secular traditions, and the other wrote its sacred history. Perhaps it is just more than mere coincidence.

After obtaining an ancient civilization's record that had been deposited in a hill near his home in Palmyra, New York, Joseph Smith, Jr. was able to begin the work of translating the Book of Mormon. The account was recorded in an ancient language, engraved on plates (sheets) of gold that were protected from exposure to the elements and other harm for over 1,400 years before Joseph Smith acquired them. The plates were concealed through the centuries in a box made of stones—cemented together, and buried to await the day when they would come forth and bring "much restoration to the house of Israel" (2 Ne. 2:24). It is the translation of these ancient plates that constitutes the Book of Mormon. Upon publication of the book, Joseph Smith proclaimed it to be "the most correct of any book on earth" ("Introduction," Book of Mormon).

The prophet Lehi pronounced a blessing upon his son, Joseph, promising him that his seed would be blessed and that they would "not utterly be destroyed" (2 Ne. 3:3). This blessing included the words of an ancient prophecy given by Joseph of Egypt. Referring to Joseph Smith, Jr., a portion of the prophecy states:

I will make for him a spokesman. And . . . I will give unto him that he shall write the writing of the fruit of thy loins, unto the fruit of thy loins, and the spokesman of thy loins shall declare it. (2 Ne. 3:18)

Some have considered that Oliver Cowdery or Sidney Rigdon may have been the spokesman referred to in this section. While it is true, several people may play the role of a temporary spokesman for a time, like Aaron was for Moses. However, just like the spiritual spokesman for Moses is the law of Moses or the Bible, the spiritual spokesman for Joseph Smith is the Book of Mormon (see 2 Ne. 3:17–22). Upon his death, the following was written about this "choice seer" of the latter days: "Joseph Smith, the Prophet and Seer of the Lord, has done more, save Jesus only, for the salvation of men in this world, than any other man that ever lived in it" (D&C 135:3). A great measure of his efforts for the salvation of men lies in the translation of the Book of Mormon.

The prophet also showed interest in the geography of the Book of Mormon. In 1841, only 11 years after the Book of Mormon was published, the works of John Lloyd Stephens were published, and they included Frederick Catherwood's artistic drawings of several ancient Mesoamerican ruins.[3] (Coincidentally, several of these sites will be mentioned later in this text as they relate to the late Nephite time period and the Maya Classic era. In the *Times and Seasons,* a newspaper edited by the Prophet Joseph Smith and published by the Church, a statement appeared which reads: "It would not be a bad plan to compare Mr. Stephens' ruined cities with those in the Book of Mormon."[4]

TIME AND PLACE

It would be a mistake to assume that the only people who ever lived in the Americas or who lived in Mesoamerica were all descendants of Lehi. The descendants of Jacob are not the only people who lived in the Middle East in ancient times, nor are the Mormons the only people who settled the West in modern times.

A comparative study of Mesoamerica's ancient cultures and those in the Book of Mormon requires a basic understanding of the civilizations that flourished during that time period. As near as can be determined, Mesoamerica's civilizations are located in the same area where the Nephites, Lamanites, and Jaredites lived out their history. However, two words must be fixed in our minds as we attempt to discover any correlation between the ancient civilizations of Mesoamerica and those in the Book of Mormon—*time* and *place*.

Most of the events in the Book of Mormon took place in the land of Nephi and the land of Zarahemla. As near as can be determined from details found both in the Book of Mormon and on the Mesoamerican map, that distance extends about 300 miles from north to south and 300 miles from east to west. We learn these dimensions from the travels of Limhi, Ammon, and Alma (see Mosiah 7–8, 18, 23–24). By referring to the Mesoamerican map and traveling through the area itself, we can also measure the topography's distance and elevation in this territory of the ancient Maya.

Artifacts show facial characteristics of two distinct civilizations: Maya and Olmec. Left insert: Sculpture made of iron and silver depicting Pacal Na, a Maya Priest/King (A.D. 603–684) from Palenque. Right insert: Photograph of large Olmec head engraved out of basalt that dates from 1200–600 B.C.

SACRED GEOGRAPHY 13

Above: The beauty of Mesoamerica is illustrated in the photo of Lake Catemaco located in the Tuxtla mountains of Veracruz, Mexico, which appears to have been in the land of Cumorah referred to by Mormon as it is close to both the Hill (Shim) and the Waters of (Ripliancum). (Mormon 6:2).

Left: The Post-Book of Mormon site of Tulum illustrated by artist Frederick Catherwood dates from A.D. 1200–1500, and illustrates the continuation of building programs and pagan worship a century after the demise of the Nephite civilization.

Most of the events described in the Book of Mormon took place from 600 B.C. to A.D. 250, or in other words, from 1 Nephi through most of 4 Nephi. This historical period in Mesoamerica is called the late pre-Classic era. Most of the Classic era (A.D. 250–900), however, and all of the post-Classic (A.D. 900–1500) postdate the history recorded in the Book of Mormon.

Many have erred when attempting to propose Book of Mormon sites because they have ignored those two principles—time and place. To label the fourteenth-century site of Tulum, or the A.D. 1200 temple of Kukulcan at Chichen Itza, or the A.D. 400–800 site of Palenque, as Book of Mormon cities does little to establish the veracity of the Book of Mormon.

The chart on the following two pages is designed to help students understand some of the major archaeological sites with their corresponding periods of occupation and building construction.

14 SACRED SITES

| 2500 BC | 2000 BC | 1500 BC | 1000 BC |

SAN JOSE MAGOTÉ, OAXACA
(OLMEC) 2600 BC–600 BC

SAN LORENZO, VERACRUZ
(OLMEC) 1500 BC–300 BC

LA VENTA, TABASCO
(OLMEC) 1500 BC–300 BC

TRES ZAPOTES, VERACRUZ
(OLMEC) 1500 BC–300 BC

IZAPA, CHIAPAS, MEXICO
(OLMEC/MAYA) 1200 BC–AD 1200

KAMINALJUYU, GUATEMALA
(OLMEC/MAYA) 1200 BC–AD 1200

> The Mulekites (or people of Zarahemla) were part of all three civilizations mentioned in the Book of Mormon: Jaredites from 500–200 B.C.; Nephites from 200 B.C.–A.D. 350; and Lamanites from A.D. 350–900.

JAREDITES

Legend:
- ■ OLMEC
- ■ OLMEC/MAYA
- ■ MAYA
- ■ ZAPOTEC
- ■ TEOTIHUACAN
- ■ TOLTEC
- ■ AZTEC

SACRED GEOGRAPHY 15

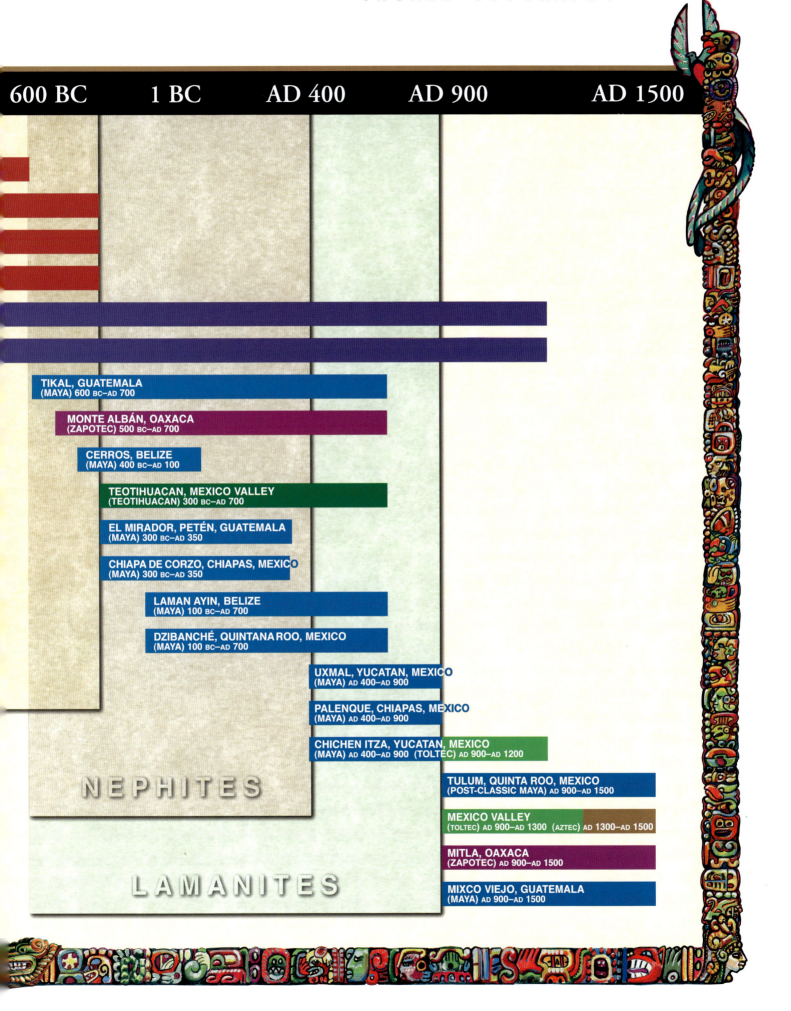

| 600 BC | 1 BC | AD 400 | AD 900 | AD 1500 |

TIKAL, GUATEMALA
(MAYA) 600 BC–AD 700

MONTE ALBÁN, OAXACA
(ZAPOTEC) 500 BC–AD 700

CERROS, BELIZE
(MAYA) 400 BC–AD 100

TEOTIHUACAN, MEXICO VALLEY
(TEOTIHUACAN) 300 BC–AD 700

EL MIRADOR, PETÉN, GUATEMALA
(MAYA) 300 BC–AD 350

CHIAPA DE CORZO, CHIAPAS, MEXICO
(MAYA) 300 BC–AD 350

LAMAN AYIN, BELIZE
(MAYA) 100 BC–AD 700

DZIBANCHÉ, QUINTANA ROO, MEXICO
(MAYA) 100 BC–AD 700

UXMAL, YUCATAN, MEXICO
(MAYA) AD 400–AD 900

PALENQUE, CHIAPAS, MEXICO
(MAYA) AD 400–AD 900

CHICHEN ITZA, YUCATAN, MEXICO
(MAYA) AD 400–AD 900 (TOLTEC) AD 900–AD 1200

TULUM, QUINTA ROO, MEXICO
(POST-CLASSIC MAYA) AD 900–AD 1500

MEXICO VALLEY
(TOLTEC) AD 900–AD 1300 (AZTEC) AD 1300–AD 1500

MITLA, OAXACA
(ZAPOTEC) AD 900–AD 1500

MIXCO VIEJO, GUATEMALA
(MAYA) AD 900–AD 1500

NEPHITES

LAMANITES

AND IT CAME TO PASS THAT I BEHELD THE ROD OF IRON, WHICH MY FATHER HAD SEEN, WAS THE WORD OF GOD, WHICH LED TO THE FOUNTAIN OF LIVING WATERS, OR TO THE TREE OF LIFE; .... THE TREE OF LIFE WAS A REPRESENTATION OF THE LOVE OF GOD. (1 NE. 11:25)

CHAPTER ONE
Lehi's Landing Site

*After we had sailed for the space of many days
we did arrive at the promised land. (1 Nephi 18:23)*

Left: Highlighted portion of map shows the proposed area where Lehi landed. It is the same place where Izapa, Stela 5, was discovered, located along the Pacific coast of Mexico near the Guatemala border and near the city of Tapachula, Chiapas, Mexico.

Opposite: Engraved, 15-ton stone monument labeled Izapa, Stela 5, located along the Pacific coast of Mexico near the Guatemala border. Engraved around 200 B.C., the same time Mosiah became king over the people of Zarahemla. Manifests Hebrew writing style. Has been proposed by some LDS scholars as a representation of Lehi's dream of the tree of life. (1 Nephi 8–11)

The Frankincense Trail

A few years ago we took a group of people through Israel, Jordan, Yemen, and Oman—following, as close as possible, the old Frankincense Trail. Our guide in Jordan kept pronouncing "frankincense" as two words, "frank-incense." Of course, it is two words. "Frank" comes from the French word *franche*, meaning, "to be honest or frank or pure." And the second half of the word refers to the fragrant "incense," a popular trading item of that day. The trade route was named after this "pure" incense, which caravan traders had moved along that old trail from Oman to Damascus for centuries. For the most part, this type of incense can only be found near the Arabian sea coast of Salalah, in the department of Dhofar. The word *dhofar* is derived from the word *ophir*, which means "abundance," or "bountiful," the same word Lehi used to describe this region 600 years before Christ. It is probable that Lehi was familiar with this route and followed it when he fled Jerusalem.

The precious frankincense also appears to be mentioned in Isaiah's prophecy, "they shall bring gold and incense" (Isa. 60:6), and was probably the very same incense delivered to Solomon by the queen of Sheba, who traveled the Frankincense Trail from Sheba to Jerusalem 300 years before Lehi. Frankincense was also one of three gifts brought to Christ by the prophets from the East (Matt. 2:1–12). However, it was highly esteemed centuries prior to both Isaiah and Christ. In the days of Moses only a mixture of frankincense, or pure incense, along with other sweet spices, could be used in the tabernacle ceremony.

And the Lord said unto Moses, Take unto thee sweet spices . . . with pure frankincense. And thou shalt make it a perfume, a confection after the art of the apothecary, tempered together, pure and holy. And thou shalt beat some of it very small, and put of it before the testimony in the tabernacle of the congregation, where I will meet with thee: it shall be unto you most holy (Ex. 30:34–36).

It was so holy that it was not to be used otherwise:

And as for the perfume which thou shalt make, ye shall not make to yourselves according to the composition thereof: it shall be unto thee holy for the Lord Whosoever shall make like unto that, to smell thereto, shall even be cut off from his people (Ex. 30:37-38).

This white resin, or fruit, which gives off a sweet aroma when burned was so precious anciently that it may have been the imagery used by Lehi when he described the fruit he saw in vision as "desirable to make one happy" and most "sweet above all." He related that the fruit thereof was white, to "exceed all whiteness" (1 Ne. 8:10–12; 11:8). The gum (fruit) of the Frankincense tree is white and reflects a bright glow when the morning sunrays fall upon it. Perhaps the tree of life, which symbolizes Jesus in Lehi's vision, looked very similar to the pure Frankincense tree. This would certainly be compatible with the sweet resin the Frankincense tree produces, paralleling the sweet, aromatic white fruit of the tree of life—a fitting symbol for the love of God. In other words, just as the frank (pure) incense was considered one of the greatest of all gifts anciently, even to the extent that it was one of the gifts delivered to the Savior at His birth, so is the love of God, even eternal life, the greatest of all gifts, eternally.

Below: The white resin, or fruit, of the Frankincense Tree from Salalah, Oman may be the imagery used by Lehi to illustrate "the fruit thereof was white" (I Ne. 8:11).

It was likely the Frankincense Trail that Lehi traveled from Jerusalem to Salalah, Oman. As we traveled this route on our journey from Nehem (Nahom), Yemen to Dhofar (Bountiful), Salalah, I was impressed with the many other images Lehi could have drawn upon to describe his vision of the tree of life, as his caravan traveled through the same desolate Empty Quarter from Nahom to Bountiful. Dr. S. Kent Brown has also had this particular impression, pointing out in one particular article various striking images that Lehi would have seen in his journey and used to reinforce his teachings. For example, Lehi and his colony would have traveled at night to avoid marauders, and it may have been comparable to the vision's "dark and dreary waste" (1 Ne. 8:7). And when they arrived at Shibam, Yemen, the Manhattan of the Arabian Desert, they would have seen a fitting image for the large and spacious building, which stood with its lights flickering in the upper stories "as it were in the air, high above the earth" (1 Ne. 8:26).[1]

After traveling eight years in the wilderness, Lehi and his colony arrived at a place called Bountiful, recorded as follows in Hebrew's beautiful poetic style:

We did come to a land which we called Bountiful,
    because of its much fruit and wild honey; and all things which were prepared
        of the Lord that we might not perish.
            And we beheld the sea, which we called Irreantum,
        which, being interpreted, is many waters.
            And it came to pass that we did pitch our tents by the seashore;
      and notwithstanding we had suffered many afflictions and much difficulty, . . .
    we were exceedingly rejoiced when we came to the seashore;
And we called the place Bountiful, because of its much fruit. (1 Ne. 17:5–6)

LEHI'S LANDING SITE 19

Top Left: Old city of Jerusalem. Lehi left Jerusalem 600 years prior to the birth of Christ (1 Ne. 10:4).

Top Center: Sinai Desert. Lehi and his colony spent eight arduous years camping and journeying in the wilderness from Jerusalem to Bountiful (proposed in the region of Dhofar, Oman) prior to their departure to the promised land (See 1 Nephi 17:4).

Top Right: Area near the Red Sea. Lehi's travels took him from Jerusalem to the region around the Red Sea where Moses and the Israelites had camped seven hundred years earlier.

Above: Camel caravan. The camel is the animal of the Arabian Desert. Our journey from Jerusalem to the Red Sea and from Yemen to Oman made us acutely aware of how arduous this journey would have been for Lehi and those who traveled with him over 2700 years ago.

Above Right: Map showing Lehi's trail from the Red Sea to the place called Bountiful following the old Frankincense trail from Jordan to present-day Oman. The names of Jerusalem, Red Sea, Nahom, and Bountiful still exist today in their proper locations.

The reason they "called" these places certain names, such as Nahom and Bountiful, is because that was in reality their respective names. It is very common in the Hebrew language to say "his name is called" as opposed to "his name is."

The next major task confronting Lehi and his family was the building of a ship and sailing to the promised land. However, after much suffering and great perseverance they did indeed arrive in "the land of their inheritance" (1 Ne. 13:30).

Izapa and the Promised Land

The mystery of where Lehi landed in the new world has been a topic of debate since the coming forth of the Book of Mormon, and includes a variety of possibilities. However, what we know today from both internal and external sources confirms that Lehi most likely landed on the Pacific side of the Americas (see Alma 22:28). Most Latter-day Saint scholars agree that Mesoamerica is the most logical candidate for the place where Lehi landed. One of the leading candidates for this landing site is the Soconusco Valley located in Chiapas, Mexico, which is close to the Guatemala border along the Pacific Ocean. It is also where the ancient archaeological zone of Izapa lies in ruins. Correspondingly, Izapa shows evidence of a written language dating to the same time period when Lehi's party arrived. Hence, the archaeological evidence is sound. And the geography of the region fits the required Book of Mormon specifications, such as a sea east and a sea west, and a narrow strip of wilderness that connects both seas (Alma 22:27).[2]

Although occupation of the Izapa area began about 1500 B.C., the period in which most of its monuments were engraved falls between 300 B.C. and A.D. 250. This is the same time span in the Book of Mormon that encompasses the books of Omni, Mosiah, Alma, Helaman, 3 Nephi, and 4 Nephi. As Latter-day Saint scholar Garth Norman points out:

> For almost a thousand years from 600 B.C. to A.D. 400, Izapa seems to have been the largest and most important center on the Pacific coast, undoubtedly serving both civil and religious functions. There is strong evidence that Izapa sculpture was primarily or entirely religious in origin and function.[3]

LEHI'S LANDING SITE

The following chart shows the dates associated with the Izapa culture as set forth by the New World Archaeological Foundation. You will observe that the early pre-Classic period corresponds with the middle Jaredite time and that the middle pre-Classic era picks up both the Mulekite and Nephite early periods.

TIME PERIOD OF IZAPA

Early Pre-Classic	1500 B.C.–850 B.C.	Middle Jaredite
Middle Pre-Classic	850 B.C.–350 B.C.	Late Jaredite, Early Nephite, Early Mulekite
Late Pre-Classic	350 B.C.–A.D. 250	Middle Nephite
Early Classic	A.D. 250–A.D. 500	Late Nephite
Middle Classic	A.D. 500–A.D. 700	Post-Nephite
Late Classic	A.D. 700–A.D. 900	Decline of Izapa
Early Post-Classic	A.D. 900–A.D. 1200	Izapa abandoned[4]

Opposite: The fertile Soconusco valley located in southeastern Mexico near the Guatemala border is proposed as the area where Lehi and his people landed as they arrived at the promised land.

Above Right: Goat water bag from Yeman. In the area of Shibam, 250 miles east of Marib (valley of Nahom), goat water bags line the hardware store walls as they are still used today for caravans traveling through the vast empty quarter of the Arabian desert.

Since Izapa was located on the southward side of the Isthmus of Tehuantepec, logic suggests that the Nephites/Lamanites mingled with a remnant of the Jaredites from approximately 600 B.C. until the Jaredite nation fell around 300 B.C.—which the Book of Mormon confirms.

During the early Classic period (A.D. 350) the Lamanites, the Gadianton robbers, and the Nephites entered into a treaty, in which the Nephites took the Land Northward (Morm. 2:28–29). It appears that as a result of this treaty, Izapa, along with other sites southward of the Isthmus of Tehuantepec, began to decline in population.

Further, if we can assume that the "place of their fathers' first inheritance" is the same place where Lehi landed, then it is clear that Lehi landed on the Pacific Coast as outlined in the following scripture:

> The Lamanites . . . were spread through the wilderness on the west, in the land of Nephi; yea, and also on the west of the land of Zarahemla, in the borders by the seashore, and on the west in the land of Nephi, in the place of their fathers' first inheritance, and thus bordering along by the seashore. (Alma 22:28)

Taking into consideration the criteria established earlier, Izapa is a leading candidate for the place where Lehi landed, or the place of Lehi's first inheritance.

22 SACRED SITES

THE TREE OF LIFE STONE

In a pasture about six miles from the Guatemalan border near the Pacific Ocean and close to the city of Tapachula, Mexico, there rests a fifteen-ton engraved stone. The stone, labeled Izapa Stela 5, whose central figure is the indigenous Ceiba tree, is flanked by other engraved monuments. All in all, over eighty monuments

Above: Over eighty engraved stone monuments have been discovered at Izapa. Occupancy at Izapa dates from 1500 B.C. to A.D. 1200. Most of the engraved stones date from 200 B.C. to A.D. 350. The inscribed stones, stelae or stela, are afforded protection from the elements by covered hutches.

Left: Izapa, Stela 5. This 15-ton stone measuring about eight feet high and five feet wide is the most intricate of all of the engraved monuments at Izapa. It was engraved c. 200 B.C. Leading Latter-day Saint scholars have suggested correlations with Lehi's family, a tree of life, filthy waters, a rod of iron, and other symbols mentioned in Lehi's dream (1 Ne. 8 & 11).

engraved with some type of writing thereon have been discovered at the ancient archaeological site of Izapa. Stela 5 attracted the attention of LDS archaeologist M. Wells Jakeman, who in the late 1940s reported a possible connection with the engravings on the stone and the symbols mentioned in Lehi's vision. His subsequent analysis of the writings on the stone and work by other archaeologists, the most prominent being V. Garth Norman, has stirred considerable interest among Latter-day Saints since its discovery. Dr. Jakeman proposed that this 200 B.C. engraving may indeed be a representation of Lehi's dream as recorded in 1 Nephi 8. Others have suggested that it may even have been commissioned by the 200 B.C. King Mosiah, and that it may have been a memorial to the first parents, Lehi and Sariah. This may account

for its location in the area that several legitimate scholars propose as the place where Lehi landed, or the land of his first inheritance (Alma 22:28). Norman portrays it as a text outlining the creation or man's journey though life—and in essence, a tree of life experience.[5]

The above interpretation has not, however, been without its critics. Hugh Nibley and John Sorenson, both prolific Book of Mormon researchers, chided Jakeman for his enthusiasm. More recently, John Clark, field director of the New World Archaeological Foundation, presented what he considered to be a more accurate drawing of the stone. He then challenged its relationship to the Book of Mormon, considering it as being more relative to the Popul Vuh, an ancient document of the Quiche Maya in Guatemala.[6]

Conversely, LDS archaeologists Bruce Warren and Richard Hauck rejected Clark's commentary and reported that there are too many consistencies with Lehi's dream for it to be coincidental.[7] According to Dr. Alan Christensen, who has presented an updated translation of the Popul Vuh, the style of writing in both the Book of Mormon and the Popul Vuh manifest the same exquisite style of Hebrew writing called chiasmus. This in turn may suggest a relationship with those two documents and Izapa Stela 5.[8]

While we may not be able to prove or disprove a firm relationship with Stela 5 and Lehi's dream, there are several things which are intriguing and perhaps even definitive. (1) The major standard of measurement on the stone, as discovered by V. Garth Norman, is the Biblical cubit,[9] and (2) the style of writing on the stone, as discovered by Todd B. Allen, manifests Hebrew chiasmus. The chiasmic pattern is as follows:

   A. Sariah figure (supporting her prophet husband)
      B. Lehi figure (a prophet)
         C. Laman figure (back to the tree)
            D. The Tree of Life (Christ)
         C. Lemuel figure (back to the tree)
      B. Nephi figure (a prophet)
   A. Sam figure (supporting his prophet brother)

The People of Nephi

The question is often asked if there were people in the promised land when Lehi arrived. From historical and archaeological evidence, the answer is yes. More specifically, if Izapa is the place where Lehi landed, were there people there when Lehi landed? Again from an archaeological and linguistic perspective, the answer is yes. It has been determined that in the region of Mesoamerica there were six major languages spoken at 600 B.C.[10] Neither Hebrew nor Egyptian is on the list.

Although it is not definitive, a careful analysis of 2 Nephi and Jacob requires the presence of more people than are named in the pilgrimage from Jerusalem to the promised land. Perhaps we should not ask *if* there were people in Lehi's promised land when he arrived, but rather, *who* were the people that were present upon the arrival of Lehi's colony. Archaeology would say the Mayans and the Olmecs. The Book of Mormon would suggest the Jaredites, or a remnant thereof. And I would propose that these are one and the same.

As near as can be determined, the Jaredites and the Nephites shared a common time period for about 300 years. Lehi arrived shortly after 600 B.C., but the Jaredite nation fell around 300 B.C. However, the Jaredites had their headquarters in the Land Northward, that is, north of the narrow neck of land, while Lehi landed in the southern area that later became part of the land of Nephi (Alma 22:28). This poses a problem in that both the land of Nephi and the land of Zarahemla were located in the Land Southward, or south of the narrow neck of land (Ether 9:31). Furthermore, the Lord brought Lehi into the land south (Hel. 6:9). The Jaredites lived

in the Land Northward and they had preserved the Land Southward as a place to hunt wild animals for food (Ether 10:21). This may suggest that there were no people living in the Land Southward when Lehi arrived. Fortunately, the book of Ether may help solve this puzzle. Between 1500–1000 B.C. when Heth was king of the Jaredites, a remnant of the Jaredites escaped from the Land Northward and went into the Land Southward.

This remnant of Jaredites who fled into the Land Southward may have been the forefathers of some of the people who the Lord prepared to accept Christ as taught by Nephi, and who became part of the Nephite kingdom. Just like Jerusalem was a land bridge for people to cross as they traveled from Egypt to Babylon, or like Salt Lake is the crossroads of the west, so was Izapa located at a crossroad. In all three cases, anyone passing through at that particular time in history would have the opportunity to receive the gospel message.

There are several sites along the southern coast of Chiapas and Guatemala that manifest a large Olmec influence between 1500–1000 B.C. Among them are Izapa, La Blanca, Abaj Takalik, El Baul, Monte Alto, and Bilbao. These sites establish a trail from Izapa to Kaminaljuyu, and the latter also shows Olmec influence prior to 600 B.C.

Above: Olmec mask from Oaxaca. The ancient Olmec civilization influenced the Mayans in the same manner in which the Jaredites influenced the Nephites. Remnants of the ancient Olmec/Jaredite nation were living along the Pacific corridor located between the proposed area of Lehi's landing and the land of Nephi which was settled by Nephi, probably present-day Guatemala City. These remnants of the Jaredites appear to have been prepared by the Lord to accept the teachings of Nephi.

Right: Local children living near the archaeological zone of Izapa display the cocoa pod. The cacoa, or cocoa beans, have a traditional high value among the people of Mesoamerica and continued through the early years of the Spanish conquest as part of their monetary trading system as opposed to coins introduced by the Spanish. For example, in the 16th century, 100 grams of cocoa beans could be traded for a healthy rabbit.

Opposite: The serpent motif is highly prevalent in Mesoamerica. The poisonous serpents referred to in the Book of Ether symbolically represent the secret combination governments that poisoned the hearts of the people (Ether 9:31).

SERPENTS AND FLOCKS

It is reported in Ether 9 that Heth became the king of the Jaredites and was directly involved with secret combinations. This stirred up the anger of the Lord, and He caused a drought to come upon the face of the land. In Ether 9, verse 31, we read the following:

> "And there came forth poisonous serpents also upon the face of the land, and did poison many people. And it came to pass that their flocks began to flee before the poisonous serpents, towards the land southward, which was called by the Nephites Zarahemla."

A careful reading of this verse may cause questions to arise. Neither serpents nor flocks behave in the manner described here. That is, poisonous serpents do not pursue animals; they defend themselves against intruders, including animals. Additionally, if in reality the flocks represent sheep or cattle, it is contrary to the way these animals react. They simply do not travel hundreds of miles just to get away from snakes. The distance under consideration is from San Lorenzo, Veracruz, located at the top of the Isthmus of Tehuantepec, to Izapa, Chiapas, or about 250 miles.

If the serpents and flocks represent groups of people instead of animals, the scripture in Ether 9:31 takes on an entirely different meaning. The poisonous serpents may be symbolic of the secret combinations, which did "poison many people" (Ether 9:31). This is exactly how secret combinations work. They spread their deadly poison among the people. They draw them away by false promises for the sole purpose of obtaining power over the masses and to get gain. Hence, the flocks could represent a righteous group of people who retreated to the Land Southward to escape the wickedness that had come upon the land. The word "flocks" is used in many instances in the scriptures to represent a righteous group of people. Indeed, the Savior is the Good Shepherd who watches over His flocks (Alma 5:59–60).

Moroni then describes what happened to the flocks: "There were many of them which did perish by the way; nevertheless, there were some which fled into the land southward. And it came to pass that the Lord did cause the serpents that they should pursue them no more" (Ether 9:32–33). The poisonous serpents, meaning the secret combination government of the Jaredites, sealed off the narrow pass to prevent other people from going into the Land Southward. The people who did escape into the Land Southward went through the narrow pass on to the archaeological sites mentioned on the previous page. Of equal interest is the term used by Moroni wherein he states that the people followed the "course of the beasts" (Ether 9:34). The word *Tehuantepec* is literally translated as "a wilderness of wild beasts," and it is this very area where the righteous group of people would have traveled to get into the Land Southward—in other words, they followed the trail of the beasts.

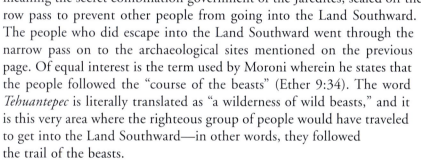

In conclusion, it appears that the Lord prepared a group of people who would receive the gospel preached by Nephi and who would go with him to the land of Nephi. Those who did not accept the gospel became known as Lamanites. As Jacob explains, they called those who were friendly towards Nephi, Nephites and those who sought to destroy the people of Nephi, Lamanites (Jacob 1:14).[11]

CHAPTER TWO
UP TO NEPHI

*They departed into the wilderness with their numbers
which they had selected to go up to the land of Nephi. (Alma 17:8)*

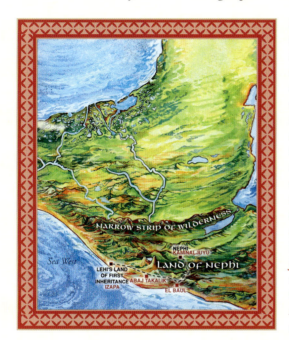

I have become impressed with the concept that it is not so much that the Book of Mormon teaches us about Mesoamerica, but that Mesoamerica teaches us so much about the Book of Mormon. By understanding the distances, directions, elevations, culture patterns and lifestyles of the colorful country and native people of Guatemala we are able to move back into the historical time tunnel of their forefathers and feel the Book of Mormon come to life. As one person put it, "prior to visiting the area, it was like seeing the Book of Mormon on stage with ill-fitted props. The experience itself was like seeing it filmed live on location." The purpose of this chapter is to provide you with a feeling of walking in the footsteps of Nephi, Abinadi, Alma, and others who walked that path over 2000 years ago.

THE LAND OF NEPHI

The Book of Mormon is consistent. Whenever movement is mentioned from the land of Zarahemla to the land of Nephi, the statement is always "up to Nephi." The fact that Nephi was south of Zarahemla (Alma 22:27) implies that the statement is referring to elevation. It appears, then, that the land of Nephi was up in the mountains. From other sources in the Book of Mormon we learn that the land/city of Nephi was also in a valley (Mosiah 7:6), that there was a sea on the east and a sea on the west (Alma 22:27), that there was a narrow strip of wilderness, or a narrow mountain range, that divided Nephi from Zarahemla (Alma 22:27), and that the distance between Nephi and Zarahemla is less than forty days (Mosiah 7:4). We also know that Nephites occupied the land from about 570 B.C. to 180 B.C.—that is, Nephi to Mosiah—and then another group of Nephites, Zeniff to Limhi, lived in the land of Nephi under Lamanite control from about 180–121 B.C.

Subsequently, we learn that the sons of Mosiah spent about 14 years, 91–77 B.C., preaching the gospel to the Lamanites who lived in the land of Nephi. We also know that Nephi built a temple, Noah built a palace, and that a written record was kept of their proceedings. Another important detail is that the Nephites lived under the law of Moses during their occupation of the land of Nephi.

With the above information, we can begin to piece together this particular geographical puzzle of the Book of Mormon. Most serious students of Book of Mormon geography see a strong relationship between the ancient archaeological site of Kaminaljuyu, which is located within the limits of Guatemala City, and the land and city of Nephi referred to in the Book of Mormon.

28 SACRED SITES

Kaminaljuyu was occupied from 1200 B.C. to A.D. 1200. The Formative, or late pre-Classic, dates within that time frame from 600 B.C. to 200 B.C., which is the early Nephite time period. There are four major reasons why Kaminaljuyu is considered to be the city of Nephi, including (1) there is evidence of a written language at the right time period, (2) there is archaeological evidence dating to the right time period, (3) there is traditional and cultural history which parallels the Book of Mormon account and, (4) the geographical makeup of the highlands of Guatemala corresponds with what is recorded in the Book of Mormon.[1]

ALTAR 10 AT KAMINALJUYU

Any candidate for the city or land of Nephi must show evidence of a high civilization along with a written language. The archaeological zone of Kaminaljuyu manifests a strong written language base several centuries prior to the coming of Christ, as portrayed on the engraved stones from the ancient site. The major writers during the early Nephite time period (600–200 B.C.) include Nephi, Jacob, Enos, Jarom, Omni, Chemish, and Amaleki. Furthermore, from 200 B.C. to the time of Christ, the Nephite written language began to circulate among the Lamanites (Mosiah 24), which is the same time period that the Maya written language became more prevalent in the region.[2] Correspondingly, it was during that 200 B.C.– A.D. 1 time span that other Nephite personalities inhabited the land of Nephi— including Zeniff, Noah, Limhi, Abinadi, Alma, Lamoni, and the sons of Mosiah.

> ALTAR 10 AT KAMINALJUYU MAY OFFER THE MOST COMPELLING LINGUISTIC EVIDENCE SO FAR THAT IT IS THE ANCIENT CITY OF NEPHI.

Altar 10 at Kaminaljuyu may offer the most compelling linguistic evidence so far that it is the ancient city of Nephi. Dr. Bruce W. Warren presented the hypothesis that this engraved stone, which manifests the year date of 147 B.C. in three different languages, as the transfer of kingship from King Noah to his son Limhi. (See Altar 10.) The engraved stone shows an upside down crown over the eye which, according to Warren, indicates the king is dead and perhaps even represents the death of the wicked King Noah himself. The symbol associated with fire is also prevalent. According to the glyphs that have been deciphered on Altar 10, it appears that 300 days after the death of the king by fire, a new king was coronated—Limhi, the son of Noah. A captivity glyph has also been interpreted with the advent of the new king. The 300 days is possibly indicative of the period of time during which Limhi had acted as the unofficial king, awaiting the New Year date of November 8 to formalize his title and position. During this same period, Limhi and his people were in bondage to the Lamanites, explaining the presence of the "captivity" glyph adjacent to the Limhi figure (Mosiah 19:28; 7:15).

King with upside down crown over eyelid. In Mesoamerican art, an upside down crown over the eyelid is indicative that the king is dead. This may be representative of the death of King Noah.

Limhi figure: Three hundred days after the death of the above-mentioned king, a new king was installed. D Bruce Warren proposed this figure as Limhi, the son o wicked king Noah (Mosiah 19:26).

Dates: All three dates on Altar 10 of Kaminaljuyu fall in the year 147 B.C. and correlate to the Noah/Limhi time period (Mosiah chapters 10–19).

The Temple of Nephi and the Ruins of Kaminaljuyu

And I, Nephi, did build a temple; and I did construct it after the manner of the temple of Solomon. (2 Nephi 5:16)

Above: The grassy mound in the center of the picture is located in the national park of Kaminaljuyu in Guatemala City and covers the ruins of an ancient building.

Insert: A model of the ancient city of Kaminaljuyu from the Miraflores Museum in Guatemala City. This city is proposed by several Latter-day Saint scholars as the city of Nephi.

If we are to attempt a correlation between Kaminaljuyu and the land of Nephi, we need to look closely at what was going on in Kaminaljuyu between 578 and 121 B.C. (that is, the Nephi to Limhi time period), which might give us a clue about Nephite culture. The above time period falls into what is called the Late Formative or late pre-Classic period of Kaminaljuyu. The Late Formative period encompasses 500 to 200 B.C., with an

estimated standard error of plus or minus 100 years. The following chart shows the Kaminaljuyu Project Culture Sequence.[3]

KAMINALJUYU PROJECT CULTURE SEQUENCE

Modern Period	A.D. 1800–1971
Colonial Period	A.D. 1500–1800
Late Post-Classic Period	A.D. 1200–1500
Early Post-Classic Period	A.D. 1000–1200
Late Classic Period	A.D. 700–1000
Middle Classic Period	A.D. 400–700
Early Classic Period (Late Nephite)	A.D. 200–400
Late Terminal Formative Period (Middle Nephite)	A.D. 1–200
Early Terminal Formative Period (Middle Nephite)	200 B.C.–A.D. 1
Late Formative Period (Early Nephite)	500–200 B.C.
Middle Formative Period	1000–500 B.C.
Early Formative Period	2500–1000 B.C.
Archaic Period	8000–2500 B.C.

In 1946, a report was published by the Carnegie Institute of Washington entitled *Excavations at Kaminaljuyu, Guatemala,* by Alfred V. Kidder, Jesse J. Jennings, and Edwin M. Shook. In reference to the discovery of these vast archaeological ruins, Kidder wrote, "Early in 1936 Licenciado J. Antonio Villacorta C., Minister of Public Education of Guatemala, asked us to investigate a mound on the Finca La Esperanza, a part of Kaminaljuyu, in which a wall had become exposed."[4] Kidder reported that the preliminary investigations at Kaminaljuyu presented evidence of it being a very old and prominent city. Throughout the years, others have echoed that same sentiment.

From 1968 to 1973, with continued consultant and administrative work, the Department of Anthropology at Pennsylvania State University conducted fieldwork at the site of Kaminaljuyu. Today, a section of Kaminaljuyu, now surrounded by the ever-growing Guatemala City, is fenced off as a national park. Several dirt mounds are visible, along with minor displays and some serious excavation works that date from 600 B.C. to A.D. 400. The detail and scholarship that go into the excavation of a site is impressive. Literally thousands of hours are spent on minute details. In the 1969 field project by Penn State, 3,000 obsidian specimens from almost all of the 550 settlement-pattern test trenches were sent to their laboratory to be analyzed for dating and ceramic comparisons.

For our purposes, however, an impressive mound excavation that existed during the late pre-Classic period (600 B.C.–A.D. 300) attracts our attention. The mound is referred to as B-V-6. Sometime between 600–400 B.C., according to the archaeologists who worked the site, the area around mound B-V-6 was transformed into a ceremonial center.[5]

The construction of B-V-6 demonstrates a great deal of sophistication in planning, workmanship, and knowledge of the problems of structural stresses involved in the erection of large conical mounds.

Other mounds dating from the early Nephite period (578–121 B.C.) also show remarkable construction patterns. In fact, of the five chronological phases that have emerged from the excavation, the first three fall within the above-mentioned time. Furthermore, on the basis of the data from the settlement pattern test trenches, the initial occupation likely occurred only shortly before mound construction began and would therefore date to 555 B.C. Jacob went up into the temple to preach to the Nephites about this same time (Jacob 2:2).

An excavated portion of Kaminaljuyu demonstrates an A.D. 400 building superimposed over a pre-Classic (Nephi) time period building. Evidence suggests that during the Nephi to Limhi time periods a special purpose building was constructed where religious activities occurred, including a ceremony of burnt offerings.

At its completion, the surface areas of what are called mounds B-V-3 through B-V-6 capped a flat area of about twenty meters in length and several meters in width. These mounds appear to demonstrate a ceremonial complex consisting of steep temple centers.[6] Additional evidence suggests that the people who occupied the area during the Late Formative period were agriculturally oriented. While not conclusive evidence, it is, nevertheless, consistent with both Nephi's and Zeniff's words (2 Ne. 5:17; Mosiah 9:9).

Evidence also exists at Kaminaljuyu indicating that special-purpose buildings were built in which certain things were burned—perhaps related to a type of ceremony. It therefore appears that the Late Formative mound complex in Finca El Mirador (Kaminaljuyu) served principally if not exclusively as a center for public religious ceremony and ritual.[7] This type of ritual sounds much like the Passover temple ceremony held in Jerusalem, which involved the burning or sacrificing of animals, in particular the lamb. All of these burnt offerings were done in similitude of Jesus Christ—who was the ultimate sacrificial Lamb. It is possible that the religious ceremonies at Kaminaljuyu which took place between 600 and 200 B.C. were those initiated by the early Nephites.

During the Formative or late pre-Classic time period at Kaminaljuyu, Jarom wrote a few words on the small plates of Nephi, confirming their observance of the law of Moses, and subsequently, animal sacrifice:

The people of Nephi had waxed strong in the land. They observed to keep the law of Moses and the Sabbath day holy unto the Lord. And they profaned not; neither did they blaspheme. And the laws of the land were exceedingly strict (Jarom 1:5).[8]

CORN AND BEANS

We began to till the ground with all manner of seeds. (Mosiah 9:9)

It's called geography by agriculture. You can actually follow the migrations of people by following their food trail, or you can eliminate areas that did not have a particular product at the time required. For example, corn is a crop that was harvested by the people of Zeniff, who lived in the land of Nephi in the second century B.C. (Mosiah 9:9). Inasmuch as corn and other products mentioned in the Book of Mormon have been grown in the highlands of Guatemala for several millennia, that helps in determining that area as a possible candidate for the land of Nephi, especially since a written language and ancient buildings, items we have already discussed, were in existence at the required time.

After Zeniff received permission from the Lamanite king to reoccupy the land of Nephi, they began to plant a wide variety of crops, including corn, wheat, barley, all manner of fruit, and two items not yet determined, *neas* and *sheum*.

> We began to till the ground, yea, even with all manner of seeds, with seeds of corn, and of wheat, and of barley, and with neas, and with sheum, and with seeds of all manner of fruits; and we did begin to multiply and prosper in the land (Mosiah 9:9; see also 9:6–7, 15).

All of the crops mentioned here are indigenous to Guatemala. It is quite amazing how many food varieties have been given to the world from the soil of Mesoamerica. Although corn is the most prominent, right behind it is beans. It is very typical for farmers to plant their corn, and when it gets to a certain height, plant the beans.

Left: A ripened field of corn also reveals an ancient engraved stone in the archaeological zone of Izapa, Chiapas, Mexico.

Below: The post-Classic ruins of Ix'imche which means corn-trees was the ancient capital of the Cachiquel Mayans and the first Spanish Capital of Guatemala.

Far Below: The colorful patchwork countryside manifests the fall colors of corn, wheat, and barley in the highlands of Guatemala near Quetzaltenango.

The cornstalks literally serve as beanpoles. Corn is illustrated on their ancient monuments, in their ancient folklore, and in their religious activities. Corn tortillas are eaten at every meal. When the local people from places like Chimaltenango go out to eat chicken at a modern fast-food place, they take their tortillas with them because the restaurants usually only serve rolls.

THE WATERS OF MORMON

As many as did believe him did go forth to a place which was called Mormon. (Mosiah 18:4)

Alma organized the Church of Christ at the Waters of Mormon, or the land of Mormon, in approximately 148 B.C. He was a priest in the court of the Nephite King Noah in the land of Nephi when the prophet Abinadi preached the gospel to Noah's kingdom and consequently suffered death by fire. Alma was converted by Abinadi's testimony and began to preach privately to the Nephites in the land of Nephi. Subsequently, Alma and his followers went forth to the place called the Waters of Mormon, which was in the forest in the land of Mormon. As we have led group tours through this region of Guatemala, two questions always seem to emerge: (1) How far are the Waters of Mormon from the city of Nephi? and (2) How large are the Waters of Mormon?

After we refer them to several Book of Mormon passages and their corresponding geographical parallels in this area, many Latter-day Saints have considered the possibility that the beautiful Lake Atitlan, located about ninety miles west of Guatemala City, is perhaps the very same Waters of Mormon we read about in the book of Alma.

Lake Atitlan is a crater, cone-type lake whose depth has not yet been revealed. It is flanked by three towering volcanoes, which manifest evidence of earthquake and volcanic activity. Remains of the ancient Mayan city Chiutinamit have even been discovered near the village of Santiago, Atitlan.[9] Today, underwater archaeology has coughed up ceramics taken out of the water base of the volcanoes. Much of the pottery dates from the late pre-Classic (600 B.C.–A.D. 300) and is the same style of pottery that has been uncovered at Kaminaljuyu, often referred to as Miraflores pottery.

That the Waters of Mormon was a beautiful place is a fact about which we *are* certain, reinforced by Alma's words expressed in poetic Hebrew fashion.

And now it came to pass that all this was done in Mormon,
>yea, by the waters of Mormon,
>>in the forest that was near the waters of Mormon;
>>>yea, the place of Mormon,
>>the waters of Mormon,
>>>the forest of Mormon,
>how beautiful are they to the eyes of them who there came to a knowledge of their Redeemer.
>(Mosiah 18:30)

This verse is an example of how a geographical setting can drive home a powerful spiritual message. Although the feelings evoked when gazing upon the beauty of Lake Atitlan are deep, they can in no way compare with the feelings that swell up in one's heart when contemplating the reality of the Atonement of Jesus Christ.

Beautiful Lake Atitlán is a leading candidate for the Waters of Mormon where Alma organized the Church of Christ in the first century B.C. (Mosiah chapter 18).

Inserts: Native Mayans who speak various dialects come from one of thirteen villages surrounding the lake. This may have been the same area where Aaron preached the gospel in the first century B.C. (Alma 21:1–13).

THEY CLAPPED THEIR HANDS FOR JOY

On one of our tours several years ago, my wife and I were walking through the marketplace at Chichicastenango, Guatemala, when a native Quiche-Mayan woman came up to us and asked, "May I be your guide to take you through the church?" She was referring to a local church where the native document, the Popul Vuh, was discovered, and we were eager to accept. Our guide not only explained various artifacts within the church, but even took us through the little museum nearby.

As we joked with her throughout, she got so excited that several times she began laughing incessantly and clapping her hands. I suddenly asked my wife, "Do you see what she's doing? Do you remember reading in Mosiah that when Alma baptized at the Waters of Mormon, they clapped their hands for joy"?

> And now when the people had heard these words, *they clapped their hands for joy;* and exclaimed: This is the desire of our hearts (Mosiah 18:11; emphasis added).

I have discovered over the years that when a particular site shows linguistic, archaeological, and geographical evidence in relation to the Book of Mormon, almost invariably a cultural statement emerges, such as is the case here. At that point, it is like going through a time tunnel back to the Nephite period and tasting just a little bit of what it would have been like.

A LAND OF PURE WATER

Alma and the members of the newly formed Church of Christ left the Waters of Mormon and traveled for eight days, an estimated distance of 64 miles, to a place they called Helam. This "pleasant land" appears to be the village of Almolonga located near the city of Quetzaltenango, Guatemala. The traveling distance is the same, the movement is in the right direction, and the name of the place is the same: *a land of pure water* (Mosiah 23:4).

Over four million native people live in the highlands of Guatemala, representing almost one-half of the population of Guatemala. Their written traditions state that they are descendants of Abraham and Jacob. Shown here is the village of Almolonga.

Insert: Friendly native Guatemala woman from Almolonga, an area proposed as the land of Helam (Mosiah 24:19), weighs out her produce using a system of weights and measures similar to what is recorded in Alma 11.

BURDENS ON THEIR BACKS

The burdens which were laid upon Alma and his brethren were made light. (Mosiah 24:15)

After living in Helam for twenty-five years, the people of Alma were discovered by an army of Lamanites who were in pursuit of Limhi, Gideon, and their guide Ammon with his sixteen men, who were taking them to Zarahemla. Amulon, who had served with Alma under King Noah and who had become a Lamanite through marriage, received permission from the Lamanite king to be the taskmaster over Alma. Amulon put tasks upon them, and the taskmasters over them prohibited them from praying to God.

And it came to pass that Amulon began to exercise authority over Alma and his brethren, and began to persecute him. And Amulon commanded them that they should stop their cries; and he put guards over them to watch them, that whosoever should be found calling upon God should be put to death (Mosiah 24:8, 11).

However, the Lord comforted Alma, saying that because of the covenant they had made with Him, He would ease the burdens placed upon their backs that they would become light and that He would deliver them from bondage. He did so by causing a deep sleep to come upon their taskmasters. After escaping, they traveled one day and arrived at a valley they called Alma (Mosiah 24:13–20), a valley that is still there today. It is in the region where the Maya Indians still carry heavy burdens on their backs.

The spiritual message is that as we journey through our wilderness of life, we too carry many weighty burdens upon our backs—the two greatest burdens being sin and death. With the help of others, and most importantly with the help of Christ, our burdens can become so light that we almost cease to feel them. It is through His Atonement that the burdens of sin and death are lifted. Our only requirement is to keep the covenants we make with Him.

Immediate left: Guatemala native from Almolonga, proposed land of Helam, carrying a bundle of grain on his shoulders.

Far left: A wood carving from the village of Santiago, Atitlán, demonstrates the heavy burdens carried by small Maya people. A leather band is placed on the forehead to help balance the load. Mormon compared the physical burdens carried by Alma's people to the emotional burdens we carry in this life. It is through Christ that these burdens are lifted.

UP TO NEPHI 41

Left: Native traditions show native women in Guatemala as they wash their clothes and then dry them along the grassy slopes. The temperature in the mountains of Guatemala are cool year-round and the need for heavy clothing is defined in the everyday living of the people as well as in the Book of Mormon (Mosiah 10:5; Alma 1:29; Helaman 6:13).

Above: Due to the heavy amount of rainfall, sugar cane is a major product of Guatemala. Daily rains occur from June through October and then the dry season sets in for six months. Over 35 volcanoes, some active, are located in the country of Guatemala.

Chapter Three
Down to Zarahemla

And they were led by the power of his arm, through the wilderness until they came down into the land which is called the land of Zarahemla. (Omni 1:13)

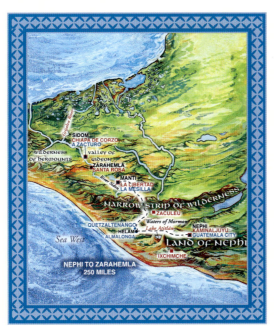

Left: Over 80% of the history in the Book of Mormon took place either in the land of Nephi or in the land of Zarahemla. The distance from Nephi to Zarahemla is approximately 28 days travel or an estimated 200 to 250 miles. Over eleven migrations mentioned in the Book of Mormon traveled the route that appears to be the same that we can travel today from Guatemala City to the state of Chiapas, Mexico.

Opposite: These rugged waterfalls that flow into Lake Atitlán reveal the stark beauty of the land between the proposed sites of Nephi and Zarahemla. The land of Zarahemla was north of Nephi and down in elevation. This is possibly where Alma and his followers hid from King Noah.

From Nephi to Zarahemla

The trip from Guatemala City to the border of Chiapas, Mexico, with stopovers at Lake Atitlan and Quetzaltenango, takes you through some of the most rugged and awe-inspiring landscape on earth. The distance is about 250 miles. The last half of the trip takes you through areas where political unrest is the norm rather than the exception. The Mam Indians have lived in the Huehuetenango region dating to 2600 B.C. As we travel through this vast, rugged wilderness, we discover we may in reality be passing through the borders between the land of Nephi and the land of Zarahemla, the same area where at least eleven migrations occurred in the Book of Mormon.

John Lloyd Stephens followed that same trail in the year 1839, and wrote of his travels from Guatemala City to Chiapas with stops at Lake Atitlan and Quetzaltenango. Throughout the centuries, it has served as the migratory route for people to travel the mountain route from Guatemala to Chiapas and from Chiapas to Guatemala. Today it is a branch of the Pan-American Highway. It now appears to be the same trail that was followed by the people of the Book of Mormon as they traveled from the land of Nephi to the land of Zarahemla and vice versa. It is these Nephite migrations recorded in the Book of Mormon that allow us to compare the distance, terrain, elevation, migration patterns, and cultural parallels of the Book of Mormon with this area today.

<u>Mosiah: From Nephi to Zarahemla c 200–180 b.c.</u>

Mosiah fled out of the land of Nephi with those who would "hearken unto the voice of the Lord" and traveled through the wilderness "until they *came down* into the land which is called the land of Zarahemla." Mosiah became king over the people of Zarahemla (Omni 1:12–19; emphasis added).

44 SACRED SITES

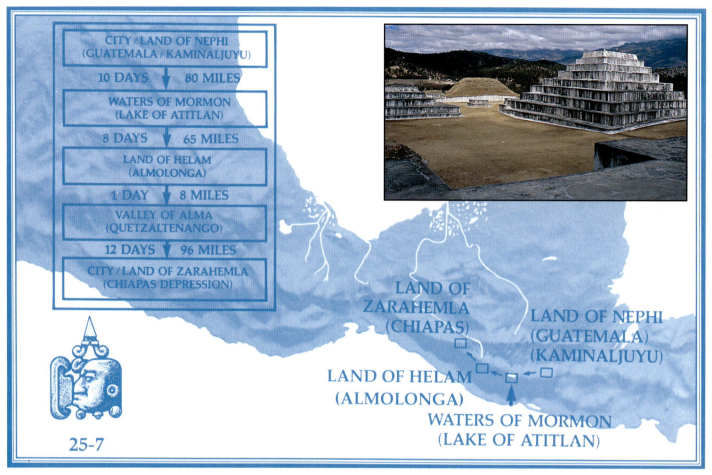

AMALEKI: FROM ZARAHEMLA TO NEPHI 200–180 B.C.

Amaleki was the record keeper who reported that after Mosiah had arrived at Zarahemla a certain number went *up into the wilderness* to return to the land of Nephi. Their leader was a stiffnecked man who caused a contention, which resulted in the death of a large number of people in the wilderness. Sadly, they never reached the city of Nephi, and only fifty people returned to the land of Zarahemla (see Omni 1:28–29).

ZENIFF: FROM ZARAHEMLA TO NEPHI C 200–180 B.C.

The same group mentioned above took additional travelers on their second journey into the wilderness. Amaleki, the son of Abinadom, said that his brother went with them. Some have suggested that his brother was none other than Abinadi who preached the gospel to the wayward Nephites in the land of Nephi. Zeniff said, "I being over-zealous to inherit the land of our fathers, collected as many as were desirous to *go up* to posses the land, and started again on our journey into the wilderness to *go up* to the land [of Nephi]" (Mosiah 9:3; emphasis added). They obtained permission from the Lamanite king, named Laman, to possess the lands of Shilom and Lehi-Nephi (Nephi). One may wonder why Zeniff was overzealous to go back up to the land of Nephi. One reason may be that it had been their homeland for 400 years. Their temple was there. It was their Jerusalem.

THE LIMHI EXPEDITION: FROM NEPHI TO ZARAHEMLA 121 B.C.

After three generations of living in what we propose to be the land of Eternal Spring (land of Nephi), the Nephites who lived under Lamanite control apparently thought freedom was better than climate. Perhaps it was similar to the following statement attributed to Heber C. Kimball. "We came to the Salt Lake Valley of our own free will, because we had to." Limhi, the son of Noah and the grandson of Zeniff, reported that he being grieved for the afflictions of his people, sent forty-three men into the wilderness to find Zarahemla and appeal to their brethren to help deliver them from bondage. They did not find Zarahemla, but discovered the

remains of a destroyed Jaredite city and twenty-four gold plates with engraving on them. More will be said about this migration in Chapter 7. The party of forty-three men returned to the city of Nephi, never having found Zarahemla (see Mosiah 8:8–12).

The Ammon Expedition: From Zarahemla to Nephi and Nephi to Zarahemla 121 b.c.

A short time after the return of the forty-three men sent by Limhi to find Zarahemla, sixteen men under the leadership of a large and strong man named Ammon were granted permission from King Mosiah, the son of Benjamin and the grandson of Mosiah. Again, the consistency of the Book of Mormon stands out. They did not know the course they should travel in the wilderness to *go up* to the land of Nephi. Remember, the land of Nephi was south of the land of Zarahemla. They wandered for forty days before they discovered the city of Shimlon in the valley of Nephi. From this statement we come to know that the distance from Nephi to Zarahemla was less than forty days' travel time. By getting the Lamanite guards drunk, Ammon led Limhi and his people down to Zarahemla to freedom (see Mosiah 7; 19–21).

Alma's Journeys: From Nephi to Zarahemla 145–121 b.c.

From Alma's travels we learn that the distance from the Waters of Mormon to Helam is only about sixty-four miles (eight days' travel), the distance from Helam to the valley of Alma is around eight miles (one day's travel), and that the distance from the valley of Alma to the land of Zarahemla is ninety-six miles (twelve days' travel). This is based on the assumption that eight miles a day is a reasonable possibility for women and children to travel through that wilderness region, also taking into account their tents and their flocks (see Mosiah 24:25). Furthermore, the distance from Nephi (Guatemala City) to the Waters of Mormon (Lake Atitlan) is about ninety miles (eleven days' travel), making their total trek from Nephi to Zarahemla less than thirty-two days, or about 250 miles. How sweet it must have been for them at their journey's end to view merciful King Mosiah who did "receive them with joy," as he had with the people of Limhi (see Mosiah 22:14; 24:25).

The Sons of Mosiah: From Zarahemla to Nephi and Nephi to Zarahemla 91–75 b.c.

Following their conversion, the sons of Mosiah elected to serve the Lord as opposed to sitting on the throne as king over Zarahemla. They *went up* to the land of Nephi to preach the word of God unto the Lamanites (see Alma 17:8). Their fourteen-year mission resulted in the conversion of a substantial number of Lamanites, who buried their weapons of war, and their sins, to embrace the gospel (see Alma 24:15–17). The converted Lamanites then returned with the sons of Mosiah to go down to Zarahemla (see Alma 27:7–8).

Opposite Map: The map illustrates the travel route from the land of Nephi to the land of Zarahemla with comparative-distance markers which correspond with the present-day map.

Opposite Inset: The post-Classic ruins of Zaculeu are nestled on the southern slope of the Cuchumatanes which divides the waters and are identified as the same mountain range that divided Nephi from Zarahemla.

Right: This Jade Olmec figure bearing a cub Jaguar may suggest the name of Shiblon, a name that Alma, who lived in the land of Zarahemla, gave to his son. Yax Balaam (first or young Jaguar) carries the same pronunciation as Shiblon.

The Chiapas Depression

The state of Chiapas is one of the largest and most beautiful states of Mexico. Its ancient history is directly connected with Guatemala, as the Mayan people, who lived in both areas, are basically the same people. Chiapas is bordered on the west by the state of Oaxaca and on the east by the Peten Rain Forest of Guatemala. Chiapas and Oaxaca are homes to a high percentage of the native population of Mexico.

There is a large central depression that is surrounded by the Guatemala mountains on the south (Cuchumatanes) and the Chiapas mountains on the north (Lacandone). The ancient ruins of Palenque are located in Chiapas and are north of the Central Depression. The ruins of Izapa, also in the state of Chiapas, are located south of the Central Depression. The Central Depression is about the size of the country of Israel. In fact, you can almost place Israel inside the Central Depression. The capital of Chiapas is Tuxtla Gutierrez with a population of about 500,000 people.

The Grijalva River has its headwaters in the Guatemala mountains and runs through the Chiapas Depression. There are four dams that have been built on the river which supply much of Mexico's electricity.

Like the highlands of Guatemala, many native people live in the mountains of Chiapas, including the Chamula, Tzoztil, and many other groups that speak native Mayan dialects and wear traditional clothing. Chiapas is proposed herein as the land of Zarahemla.

Right: The large lagoons located in the Mexican states of Tabasco and Campeche are proposed as the "land among many waters" referred to in Mosiah 8:8.

Below: The majestic 12,000-foot mountain range that divides Guatemala from Chiapas and runs east to west is a strong possibility as the narrow strip of wilderness referred to in Alma 22:27.

DOWN TO ZARAHEMLA

The difference in elevation between what we read about the land of Nephi and the land of Zarahemla is consistent with the highlands of Guatemala and the Central Depression of Chiapas. Kaminaljuyu (Guatemala City) is 4800 feet above sea level with heights reaching 10,000 feet in the highlands. On the other hand, the Central Depression of Chiapas ranges from 1100 to 1700 feet above sea level, much lower. As mentioned previously, the Book of Mormon consistently refers to the land of Zarahemla as "down" from the land of Nephi, even though Zarahemla is north of Nephi. And every movement from Zarahemla to Nephi is described as going "up," even though Nephi is south of Zarahemla. We must thus conclude that the land of Nephi was in the mountains and the land of Zarahemla was at a lower elevation.

THE NARROW STRIP OF WILDERNESS

The east-west mountain range that extends from the Atlantic Ocean to the Pacific Ocean.

Probably the most significant geographical detail included in the Book of Mormon is a narrow mountain range that runs east to west and touches both oceans. It is like a massive wall dividing one land from another. Most of the history of the Book of Mormon took place between Nephi and Zarahemla and they are only about 250 miles apart.

The text states that the Lamanites were divided on their north from the Nephite land of Zarahemla "by a narrow strip of wilderness, which ran from the sea east even to the sea west" (Alma 22:27). This appears to be the dramatic, narrow mountain range that today divides the highlands of Guatemala from Chiapas, Mexico. Justification for the narrow strip of wilderness to be this mountain range is two-fold. (1)

The elevation difference between the land of Nephi and the land of Zarahemla requires the water to flow from south to north, which is what the Grijalva River does, and, (2) there also appears to be a mountain range in this area which would fit the Book of Mormon description.

There is a spiritual parallel to the narrow strip of wilderness that divided the land of the Lamanites from the land of the Nephites. In our own lives, there seems to exist a similar line between good and evil, and we must choose daily what side we are going to be on. If we cross over that narrow line, we risk the chance of stumbling and falling down the mountainside into Lamanite territory.

Right: The "narrow strip of wilderness" from the Zarahemla side.

Far Right: Chamula Indians near San Cristobal de las Casas, Chiapas, Mexico, (the proposed area of ancient Zarahemla) maintain the "native traditions of their fathers," a term common to the Book of Mormon.

Below: The Grijalva River begins in the mountains of Guatemala and flows through the Chiapas depression of Mexico and empties into the Gulf of Mexico. It is considered in this text as the Sidon River.

THE RIVER SIDON

*The Amlicites came upon the hill Amnihu, which was east of the river Sidon,
which ran by the land of Zarahemla. (Alma 2:15)*

The most prominent river in the Book of Mormon is the River Sidon. The Central Depression of Chiapas manifests occupation and building activity dating back to the Jaredite era. An incredible amount of building also took place during the Nephite time period from 300 B.C. to A.D. 350, all along the Grijalva River.

Some students of the Book of Mormon have considered the Usumacinta River which divides Chiapas from Peten, Guatemala, to be the River Sidon mentioned in the Book of Mormon. However, the lack of ancient ruins along the Usumacinta dating to the Nephite time period and the abundance of ancient ruins along the Grijalva River in Chiapas would favor the Grijalva as a more viable candidate for the River Sidon. In contrast, it wasn't until the Classic period around A.D. 400 that cities along the Usumacinta River began to emerge.

However, it is not just the presence of a river that determines the location of the land of Zarahemla. It is the dating of the sites along the river that is supremely important in our study. And it is the relationship with the land of Nephi as it interacted with Zarahemla that is of supreme importance. By making a preliminary assessment that Chiapas was the land of Zarahemla from c 600 B.C.–A.D. 400, we can test our Sidon/Grijalva hypotheses against other Book of Mormon statements dealing with the land of Zarahemla. This we will now do.

WILDERNESS OF HERMOUNTS

*[It] was called the wilderness of Hermounts; and it was that part of the wilderness
which was infested by wild and ravenous beasts. (Alma 2:37)*

Alma chapter 2 records a great war between Alma and Amlici, who wanted to be king and appealed to the Lamanites for assistance. A battle ensued on both sides of the River Sidon near the city of Zarahemla. Alma and his soldiers were able to cut off the Lamanites and Amlicites to the point that they did not capture the city of Zarahemla, nor could they retreat back up into the Guatemala mountains. Instead, they were driven by Alma and his military northwest of Zarahemla.

Assuming that the city of Zarahemla is located in the Chiapas Depression, then the wilderness of Tehuantepec is the wilderness referred to in Alma 2:37, the wilderness of Hermounts. This area was located northwest of Zarahemla in the same way that Tehuantepec is northwest of the Chiapas Depression today. Furthermore, there is a significant name correlation between Tehuantepec and Hermounts. They both mean "wilderness of wild beasts."

ALMA'S MISSIONARY JOURNEY

We learn a great deal about the geography of the land of Zarahemla from Alma's missionary journeys. Alma had been appointed to be the first chief judge, following the reign of three Nephite kings who had ruled in the land of Zarahemla. The kings were Mosiah, Benjamin, and Mosiah. Alma served as chief judge for eight years from 91 B.C. to 83 B.C. The main event that Mormon records about the reign of Alma is a great war between Amlici and Alma where "thousands and tens of thousands of souls" were sent to the eternal world (Alma 4:26). Alma's reign is recorded in Alma chapters 1–4. Alma had also been appointed and consecrated the high priest over the people of the Church of Christ by his father, whose name was Alma, who organized the Church of Christ at the Waters of Mormon. At the end of eight years, Alma appointed the "wise man" Nephihah, who was one of the elders of the Church, to replace him as the chief judge. This Alma did so that he could go among the people himself to preach the gospel.

City of Zarahemla and the Valley of Gideon

Alma's missionary journey began in the city of Zarahemla. He then traveled east of the River Sidon to the valley of Gideon, after which he returned to Zarahemla and rested from his labors for a time. John Sorenson

proposed the ruins of Santa Rosa to be the ancient city of Zarahemla. If this is true, then either the Loma Larga Valley or the Teopisca Valley above the Chiapas Depression are good candidates for the valley of Gideon. We get further help regarding the location of Gideon from the events of the Amlicite war (Alma 2) as it relates to the land of Minon, and the positioning of Manti with the valley of Gideon as spelled out in Alma 17:1. (See map.)

LAND OF MELEK

A year after Alma relinquished the judgment seat, he resumed his missionary labors (trace mission on map). This time he took his journey west of the River Sidon "on the west by the borders of the wilderness" (Alma 8:3–4). There are several archaeological sites which date to the first century B.C. located in the mountains west of the Grijalva River and which are close to the Pacific Ocean, the most conspicuous being Tonala and Perseverancia. It appears that Melek was involved with the fortification line that ran from the mountain to the ocean. The converts of the sons of Mosiah (Anti-Nephi-Lehies) initially settled in the land of Jershon located near the east sea (see Alma 27:22), but were subsequently moved to Melek (Alma 35:13), which was near the west sea (Alma 53:8, 22). It was that move from Jershon to Melek that caused the sons of Helaman, or the sons of the converted Lamanites, to fight near the west sea.

LAND OF AMMONIHAH

Alma next preached the gospel at Ammonihah. It was located three days' distance, a projected twenty-four miles north of Melek. The pre-Classic archaeological zone of El Mirador (not to be confused with the El Mirador site in northern Peten, Guatemala), located near Cintalapa, Chiapas, is a suggested candidate for the city of Ammonihah where Alma and Amulek preached the gospel as outlined in Alma chapters 8–14. It is in this section that we read about the Nephite monetary system. It is also the wicked city of Ammonihah that was attacked and destroyed by the Lamanites (see Alma 25:2), at the same time

the sons of Mosiah were preaching the gospel among the Lamanites. There may be a little poetic justice here. Wicked people not only destroy righteous people; they also destroy other wicked people.

Land of Sidom

Alma and Amulek, along with those who believed in their words, ended up at a place called Sidom, which may be the modern-day city of Chiapa de Corzo, located near the capital city of Tuxtla Gutierrez, Chiapas. The ancient

Opposite: Overlooking the Grijalva valley; often called the central depression of Chiapas. Late pre-Classic sites 300 B.C.–350 A.D. filled this area 150 miles long by 25–50 miles wide. The archaeological evidence presents a convincing case for the land of Zarahemla.

Left: Chiapa de Corzo. Believed to be the city Sidom mentioned in Alma chapter 15. Oldest long count date of December 9, 36 B.C., discovered here.

Below: The palace of Palenque is located in the state of Chiapas; however, the building was constructed after the close of the Book of Mormon era.

name for the city of Chiapa de Corzo is *Zactún,* which is a Mayan word meaning "white" or "limestone." By the same token, "Sidom" is an old-world name that also means "white limestone." There is a great abundance of limestone in and around the city of Chiapa de Corzo. In fact, there is a factory nearby that is used to manufacture white plasterboard today. White limestone is also used as a foundation for the roads and highways in the area.

The New World Archaeological Foundation, funded by Brigham Young University, excavated the ruins of Chiapa de Corzo in the 1960s and 70s. Archaeologists, under the direction of Gareth Lowe, discovered the oldest existing Maya long-count date yet discovered. The inscriptions bear the date of Dec. 9, 36 B.C. This is about forty-six years after Alma, Amulek, Zeezrom, and the Christians who had been ostracized from Ammonihah escaped to Sidom.[1]

WEIGHTS AND MEASURES

They did not reckon after the manner of the Jews who were at Jerusalem; neither did they measure after the manner of the Jews. (Alma 11:4)

The native Mesoamericans traded with cocoa beans, quetzal feathers, and copper figures—making transactions with a weight-and-measure system that is still utilized today. On one of our trips in 1989, we were traveling toward Guatemala City when Dean Williams, an attorney who was a member of the tour group, was reading in Alma 11 about the conversion of the lawyer Zeezrom. He asked me if there had ever been any coins discovered in Mesoamerica, to which I confirmed that there had not been. Some items made of copper have been discovered, but coins patterned with what we are familiar have not.

As we examine statements in the Book of Mormon about the Nephite monetary system it becomes clear that these verses are not describing coins. They are describing a system of weights and measures similar to what existed in the old world at the time of Lehi's departure from Jerusalem. They are perhaps comparable to weights and measures still found in Yemen. The fact that the word "coin" is inscribed in the heading of Alma chapter 11 and in the index under "senine" only suggests that it is rather common for us to think in terms of our own culture, as both the headings and index were inserted in the current revisions of the Book of Mormon. The context of the Nephite monetary system is recorded in Alma 11 as follows:

> Now these are the names of the different pieces of their gold, and of their silver, according to their value. And the names are given by the Nephites, for they did not reckon after the manner of the Jews who were at Jerusalem; neither did they measure after the manner of the Jews; but they altered their reckoning and their measure, according to the minds and the circumstances of the people, in every generation, until the reign of the judges, they having been established by king Mosiah (Alma 11:4).

There is a system of weights and measures that is still used today throughout Mesoamerica in the local markets to determine the weight and value of the item that is being sold. Of course, once a possible correlation with these and the Book of Mormon emerged, an item called *marcos* (weights) has become an essential on the Latter-day Saint shopping list. These weights consist of four small cups and a small, solid cap—each weighing differing amounts.[2] The cups nestle inside one another, much like the measuring cups we use in our American kitchens, and the small, solid cap fits inside the smallest cup.

DOWN TO ZARAHEMLA 53

Above: Guatemala women display their goods. Potatoes are grown in the higher climate. Pineapple are grown along the coast and the lower elevations, and corn is grown in both the coastal region and the highlands.

Right: Today the people only use weights to determine the price of what they sell. They are called "marcos." The configurations are similar to that which is described in Alma 11.

Senine   Seon   Shum   Limnah
ALMA 11:
5 Now the reckoning is thus—a senine of gold, a seon of gold, a shum of gold, and a limnah of gold.

CHAPTER FOUR
THE EAST WILDERNESS

And it came to pass that Moroni caused that his armies should go forth into the east wilderness; yea, and they went forth and drove all the Lamanites who were in the east wilderness into their own lands, which were south of the land of Zarahemla. (Alma 50:7)

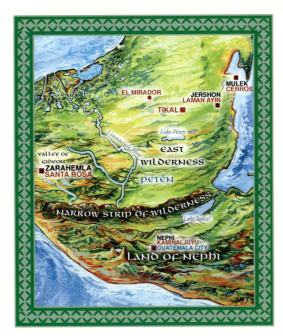

Left: In the first century B.C. the military leader Moroni led his armies into the wilderness east of Zarahemla and drove the Nephites south up into their own lands. This homestead act paved the way for many cities to be built and occupied by the Nephites. This chapter outlines the activities that took place in the East Wilderness, beginning at the above-mentioned time period.

Opposite: The ancient city of Tikal was occupied as early as 600 B.C. and continued until about A.D. 900 when it was abandoned. The pyramid shown here dates to about A.D. 600. The Nephites appear to have occupied Tikal from 100 B.C. to 350 A.D. There is not enough information in the Book of Mormon to determine the Book of Mormon name for Tikal.

THE EAST WILDERNESS AND THE PETÉN JUNGLE

In 1965, I was enrolled in a class on Book of Mormon geography under the direction of Dr. Wells Jakeman who was the first chair of the BYU Archaeology Department. I can still remember his statement: "A great key to understanding the Maya nation would be uncovered if we could determine why they settled in the jungle lowlands of Guatemala." The Petén Jungle on the Guatemala panhandle is truly a hot, humid rainforest from May to October. Throughout the entire year, it is a dense jungle filled with all manner of wildlife, including snakes, monkeys, jaguars, ocelots, and beautiful birds.

The Book of Mormon provides us with a very adequate solution as to why the people settled the area in question. Alma 22 helps us to understand that boundaries had been established between the Lamanites and the Nephites. Basically, it appears that the highlands of Guatemala were considered Lamanite territory and the lowlands of Guatemala, of which until recent years both the state of Chiapas in Mexico and the small country of Belize were a part, belonged to the Nephites.

We have location, dating, and motive for the lowlands under discussion as belonging to the 72 B.C. Nephites. If the land of Zarahemla was located in the Central Depression of the state of Chiapas, then it is fairly obvious that the East Wilderness would be what is now called the Petén Jungle of Guatemala in the current country of Belize. The lowlands are directly east of Chiapas. Belize borders what would be the eastern seashore in this same directional analysis. The dating of the archaeological sites in the area is testimony that people inhabited the area at the required 72 B.C. time period. Defensive earthworks also bear witness to the cultural patterns in existence in the East Wilderness at the time Moroni was fighting the Lamanites.

I propose that the reason the Petén Jungle was settled was to establish adequate and legitimate boundaries. The Nephites were almost completely surrounded by the Lamanites (see Alma 22:29, 34). The threat of total enclosure by the Lamanites was likely a major concern for the Nephites, who lived in the isolated land of Zarahemla. In essence, Moroni initiated a homestead act to get the Nephites to move into the East Wilderness of the Petén Jungle and Belize. The verses that justify that the settlement of the East Wilderness was a homestead act are as follows:

The Jaguar is the most feared predator in the rain forests of Guatemala. The ancient Mayans used their skin for clothing and prestige. Animal names are prevalent among the Maya and are also reflected in the Book of Mormon. Balam (Jaguar) may be the same as the cognate "Blom" in the name Shi-Blom.

> And it came to pass that Moroni caused that his armies should go forth into the *east wilderness;* yea, and they went forth and drove all the Lamanites who were in the *east wilderness* into their own lands, which were south of the land of Zarahemla. And the land of Nephi did run in a straight course from the east sea to the west.
>
> And it came to pass that when Moroni had driven all the Lamanites out of the *east wilderness,* which was north of the lands of their own possessions, *he caused that the inhabitants* who were in the land of Zarahemla and in the land round about should go forth into the *east wilderness,* even to the borders by the *seashore,* and possess the land. (Alma 50:7–9; emphasis added)

Therefore, Petén and Belize would obviously constitute the East Wilderness if the Central Depression of Chiapas is the land of Zarahemla. All directional statements are accurate to the detail in reference to both the proposed Zarahemla and the proposed land of Nephi.

THE EAST WILDERNESS 57

DEFENSIVE EARTHWORKS

Because he was a military leader himself, the author Mormon must have identified with the first-century B.C. military leader, Moroni. He even gave his son the same name. Mormon wrote that Captain Moroni was a man of "perfect understanding," and that if all men were like him, the devil would never have power over the hearts of the children of men (Alma 48:11–17).

Moroni was not only a great military leader and a man of supreme character, he was also a phenomenal innovator. One of the most significant military contributions he made was to construct defensive earthworks around the cities, which literally transformed them into forts or strongholds. The city of Bountiful, which was near the city of Mulek, also became an "exceeding stronghold" as Moroni caused the Lamanite prisoners to build a breastwork of timbers upon the inner bank of the ditch and to cast up dirt out of the ditch against the breastwork of timbers (Alma 53:4).

Left: Kings are represented on the walls of the pyramids in the Petén of Guatemala and Belize, and date to both Book of Mormon and post-Book of Mormon periods.

Above: The 100 B.C. building at Laman Ayin located in northern Belize along the New River, which may have been in the land of Jershon, where the converted Lamanites settled for a short time.

Not only was he skilled in defending Nephite cities, but he was also good at recovering them. Reclaiming Mulek was one of Moroni's greatest victories over the Lamanites, which was one of the strongest holds of the Lamanites in the "land of the Nephites."[1] But these attempts to salvage their hostage cities were not always successful. Moroni was so good at what he did that when the Lamanites and "their numberless hosts" were able to gain control of a Nephite city that had been strongly fortified by Moroni's earlier efforts, it was difficult to retake it (Alma 51:26–27).

One extremely exciting discovery in the area of the Petén, Belize, and Southern Yucatan is the possible remains of these ancient fortifications. Tikal, Becán, Cerros, Lamanai, and Dzibanche all show evidence of being fortified "after the manner of the fortifications of Moroni."

TIKAL

Regarding the ruins of Tikal, a report by two archaeologists, Puleston and Callender, in the mid 1960s revealed defensive earthworks at that ancient city. They wrote:

Fortified earthworks patterned after the style of Moroni's fortification have been discovered at several places in Petén, Guatemala, Belize, and the southern Yucatan peninsula. The mote at Becán, shown above, fits the pattern of these fortifications.

For weeks, months, and even years one spends carrying out fairly routine work there is always the possibility of stumbling onto something important that is totally unexpected. The discovery of what appears to be a 9 km long defensive earthwork 4.5 km north of the Great Plaza of Tikal is an example of just such a chance.

The earthworks lie directly between Tikal and the nearest largest site, Uaxactun. These two sites are about five hours apart in terms of walking distance; the earthworks are one hour's walk north of Tikal. Frankly, a defensive barrier of this magnitude, or for that matter of any magnitude, was not one of the things we expected to find in the process of a project to explore the outlying areas of Tikal.

At first we considered the possibility that it might have served as a canal in a water distribution system of some kind. However, this intriguing idea had to be rejected on the basis of two factors, both of which preclude the possibility that the trench could have held water: first, the extremely porous nature of limestone bedrock; and second, the way in which the trench goes up and down the sides of large hills without changing depth.

The trench is the most prominent feature of the earthworks. Its potential as a barrier to human movement was obvious. Though we didn't know its depth before we began excavation, the four-meter width of the trench posed an obstacle few Maya could have crossed by jumping. They would have had to jump upwards, as well as across the trench, to get into the embankment which abutted the south lip.[2]

Becán

Regarding defensive earthworks at Becan, David Webster wrote,

> Whatever uniqueness these conditions suggest is probably more reflective of our inadequate archaeological knowledge than any sort of new event or process in lowland civilization. After all, several apparent fortifications utilizing the earthwork principle have cropped up recently. I suspect that the ditch-embankment type of defensive system is of great antiquity in the lowlands because of its advantages of simplicity, adaptability, and efficient use in conjunction with timber palisades.

Lamanai and the People of Ammon

Belize is a small country with a population of less than 150,000, which seems out of sync with the rest of Mesoamerica. From the time of the Spanish conquest it has gone through a series of major political changes. The Mayans who lived in the area at the time of the conquest fled deep into the Petén Forest, west of Belize. Spain then passed that small section of land to the English pirates in exchange for freedom on the seas, making English the semi-official language. It then became known as British Honduras. It is interesting to note that even though Belize now has its independence, Guatemala still claims it as hers.

Belize is home to a wide variety of nationalities. Slave trade from Africa and migrations from Honduras have brought two different races of Blacks, and civil unrest in other Central American countries has caused Hispanics to seek refuge within its borders. In addition, numerous Taiwanese have found a safe haven here as well. In the past century, Mennonites with ties to Mexico, Canada, and Germany have also moved into Belize and now constitute ten percent of the population. Americans have also come to Belize for the scuba diving, to

visit the ancient Mayan ruins, and to retire. This small piece of land has been home to ancient cultures as well. I propose that this area played a major geographical and political role among the Nephites, Lamanites, and Mulekites from the second century B.C. to A.D. 400.

There is an archeological site in northern Belize called Lamanai, which apparently made a great impact on the Book of Mormon stage in the middle of the first century B.C. The name is highly suspect since Laman and Lamoni are both Lamanite king names. It is very probable that Laman, like Nephi, became a title as well as a name. In the Mayan language, the word appears to be *Laman Ayin*. While *Laman* is associated with water and *Ayin* is linked with crocodile, the meaning of the two words combined is usually referred to as "Submerged Crocodile." Moreover, one of the later rulers of Tikal was named *Yax Nun Ayin*, or "First Crocodile." It is significant to note that the word *Laman* is also associated with water in the Book of Mormon. You will recall that Lehi named a river after his son Laman and desired that he might be like that river, continually running into the fountain of all righteousness (see 1 Ne. 2:9).

The crocodile is found in many rivers and swamp areas in Chiapas, Petén, Guatemala, and Belize. It may be associated with the name of Laman. The archaeological site of Laman Ayin is translated as "submerged crocodile," and a recent drawing of Izapa, Stela 5, depicts a crocodile next to the "Laman" figure.

However, it is the location and the dating of Lamanai that makes this site a strong candidate for the land of Jershon. The dating of a major building at Lamanai places this site in the middle of the first century B.C., which, incidentally, corresponds with the same time period as its close neighbor, Cerros. In addition, Lamanai is located near the east sea, another factor which strengthens this hypothesis. Once the Anti-Nephi-Lehies crossed into Nephite territory, the Nephites gave the converts the land of Jershon, a Biblical name that means "a stranger in a strange land." The land of Jershon was on the east, located by the east sea, and joined the city Bountiful on the south. The Chief judge Nephihah placed his armies between the land Jershon and the land Nephi in order to protect these new converts from warfare (see Alma 27:22–23). As appears to always be the case, even today, that area is difficult to defend. Within a short time, the people of Ammon were transferred to Melek which is near the west sea, a distance of over 300 miles (see Alma 35:13). But as for Laman Ayin, it dates to the right time period and is in the right place, making it a strong possibility for the land of Jershon. The same is true of the archaeological site of Cerros, located in northern Belize. An attempt to establish kings at that site corresponds to the middle of the first century B.C., the same time that kingmen arose in the Book of Mormon, and in the same area.

60 SACRED SITES

Above: Banana tree flower. Bananas are grown throughout the coastal area and the jungle lowlands of Mesoamerica.

Top right: Above the jungle canopy at Tikal. This massive rain forest was the home to several million Mayans at the height of their population in the 6th century A.D. Today, less than one million people live in the department of Petén in Guatemala.

Right: Flowers and all manner of vegetation grow in abundance in the area proposed as the East Wilderness of Zarahemla. The jungle rains bring deadly mosquitoes as well as a variety of medicinal plants that "remove the cause of diseases, to which men, [are] subject by the nature of the climate" (Alma 46:40).

Opposite: Guatemala Jade is recognized worldwide for its abundance and quality. During the Classic Maya period, the priests were buried with jade masks covering their faces, and jade necklaces are a common item found in the graves.

THE CLIMATE ALLEGORY

Climate can also help us understand geography—and the climate in Mesoamerica is very distinct. Because springtime in the Rockies differs very much from April and May in Mayan country, it's a hard sale to convince people that these are the hottest months of the year. Weather in this area is distinguished by a "rainy" season and a "dry" season. When the rains begin in June, everything turns green and the temperature cools down considerably. The rains dwindle at the end of October and then the dry season begins, with occasional exceptions. As for the temperature, the mountains are always cooler than the coastal and jungle areas. The careful reader will notice that heat is mentioned in the Book of Mormon, but cold is not. Similarly, rain is mentioned, and yet snow is not.

Understanding Mesoamerica's climate greatly enhances numerous accounts in the Book of Mormon. For example, after a season without any rain, Nephi, who lived in Zarahemla or in the Chiapas Depression, prayed to the Lord to "send forth rain upon the face of the earth, that she may bring forth her fruit, and her grain in the season thereof" (Hel. 11:13). Because the Central Depression of Chiapas operates strictly under the rule of a very predictable dry and rainy season, this downpour would have been a great miracle.

When describing the conditions they suffered while fighting in the East Wilderness, Moroni uses phrases such as, the "heat of the day" (Alma 51:33) and "fevers in the land" (Alma 46:40). This describes very accurately the conditions in the rain forest of the Petén Jungle of Guatemala today. There is heat, there is rain, and consequently, there are fevers in the land—more particularly in the rainy season.

Even though the oft-stated purpose of the Book of Mormon is to bring people to Christ, Alma 46:39–41 is a well-known passage that gives certain clues about the Book of Mormon climate. If Mormon repeatedly emphasized that he couldn't include even a hundredth part of several very spiritual events (see W of M 1:5; Hel. 3:14; 3 Ne. 5:8; 26:6), why would he take up precious space on the plates to tell us about something as trivial as weather?

It must be remembered that Alma 46 is primarily a spiritual account of a righteous man rallying the people to defend their freedoms. To conclude such a powerful chapter with an almost passing remark about the weather seems a little out of place. And yet the experienced Book of Mormon student will notice the style in which these verses are written, Chiasmus. This poetic, Hebrew form is often used to underscore a spiritual lesson—and it so happens that these last few verses use that very pattern.

Because we have been given the Book of Mormon to teach us about Christ, we should expect that Mormon included this passage to achieve that end. The scripture refers to the fact that many people died. Some of them died because of the diseases to which men were subject because of "the nature of the climate." Others died of old age. Regardless of how we die, we will all die physically, simply because of our mortal condition, or "the nature of the climate."

However, God has prepared "many plants and roots . . . to remove the cause of diseases." Although we must die physically, it will not be forever, for we are not in any way compelled to die spiritually. God prepared the plants and roots, even His Only Begotten Son, to cure our mortal ailments, or sins of the flesh. In other words, He "prepareth a way for our escape from the grasp of this awful monster; yea that monster, death and hell, which I call the death of the body, and also the death of the spirit" (Alma 9:10).

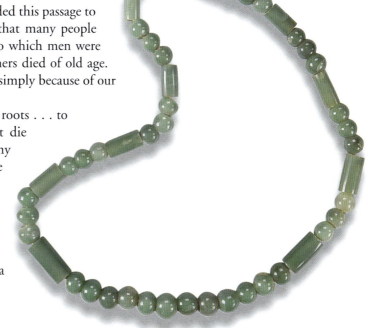

Chapter Five
The Land of Bountiful

The land on the southward was called Bountiful. (Alma 22:31)

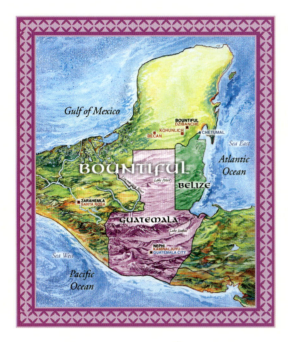

Left: The experience at Bountiful is the pinnacle of the Book of Mormon. The location is insignificant compared to what occurred there with the appearance of the Savior to the Nephites. Nevertheless, the melodic sounds of the birds ascending from the towering trees which sway gently in the breeze provide an atmosphere of sacredness that touches the hearts of those who contemplate the words, "I am Jesus Christ, whom the prophets testified shall come into the world" (3 Ne. 11:10). The purpose of this chapter is to provide the reader with information about the country, land, and city of Bountiful from both an archaeological and historical point of view.

Opposite: Bountiful was the name where Nephi built and launched the ship that carried them to the promised land. Several centuries later, the Nephites named the general land where they lived Bountiful. Today the name Tula, which has been translated as Bountiful, surfaces in many areas of Mesoamerica. An abundance of natural flowers and colorful vegetation covers the landscape.

Bountiful, the Country

Most references in the Book of Mormon refer to the land Bountiful and the land Desolation in relation to each other, such as "the land on the northward was called Desolation and the land on the southward was called Bountiful" (Alma 22:31; see also Alma 22:29–30, 32; 63:5; 3 Ne. 3:23). The term "Bountiful" appears to be synonymous with the Land Southward. This association is consistent with the Spanish Chronicles, which state that the second settlers from the time of the giants called the general area Tollan (Tula). *Tula* means "place of reeds," "land of abundance," or "Bountiful."[1]

There was a small neck of land, or an isthmus, that divided the Land Southward, Bountiful, from the Land Northward, Desolation (see Alma 22:32). Ether 9:32 states that the Nephites called the Land Southward, Zarahemla. This is not problematic, however, since the portion of "the land southward" in this particular verse refers to where the land of Zarahemla was located. On the other hand, that does not preclude the fact that Zarahemla was equivalent to a state, in the general area or country of Bountiful.

This rationale suggests that Bountiful in the Book of Mormon was not only a city and a state, but also served as an umbrella over the entire Land Southward and thereby functioned as a country. For example, the land/state of Zarahemla, and the land/state of Bountiful were both probably lands or states within the country, or general area, of Bountiful.

This thinking is consistent with Mesoamerican culture today. The state of Veracruz, the state of Oaxaca, and the state of Mexico are all states within the country of Mexico. And the principal city of each of these states bears the same name, just as the city of Nephi, the city of Zarahemla and the city of Bountiful carried the names of the larger land areas. Bountiful was also the name of the area where Lehi and his caravan arrived in the old world prior to setting sail for the promised land (see 1 Ne. 17:5).

Mormon does a masterful job of word play with Desolation and Bountiful. Alma 22:27–34 is written in exquisite Hebrew chiasmic style and presents us with a multitude of word parallels or contrasting word parallels, such as sea east and sea west, land of Nephi and of Zarahemla, and the land Desolation and the land Bountiful. We may ask ourselves the question, where would we rather live, Desolation or Bountiful? The answer is obvious. Even some of the wild animals left the Land Northward (Desolation) to go to the Land Southward (Bountiful) for food (see Alma 22:31). This required that they travel through the Isthmus of Tehuantepec, or through the trail of the beasts, to get to Bountiful (see Ether 9:34). We may also have to travel through a narrow pass as we negotiate the wilderness of mortality, and we are often pursued by our own wild beasts of temptation and sin. But this difficult journey will one day be worth all the effort once we reach the land Bountiful, or eternal life (see 2 Ne. 9:10).

BOUNTIFUL, THE CITY AND STATE

Above: The most impressive thing to me about Dzibanche is the multitude of peaceful groves surrounding the ruins, with ample room to walk among the lofty trees.

Opposite top: Classic building at Dzibanche. Means, "writing on wood," named after the engraved wooden lintels that can still be detected over some of the doorways of the buildings. This large city along with its neighbor Kohunlich was a megalopolis dating from the first century B.C. to A.D. 800.

Opposite bottom: Classic buildings cover pre-Classic buildings. A wall can still be seen that was built around the ancient city. Its close proximity to the archaeological site of Cerros, located in northern Belize, makes it a viable candidate for the city of Bountiful (Alma chapters 51 & 52).

Three ancient Book of Mormon cities, spaced out between several hundred years, share an important common denominator. The city of Nephi is first mentioned in 2 Nephi chapter 5 and dates to about 580 B.C. The city of Zarahemla is first mentioned in Omni and dates to about 200 B.C. The city of Bountiful is first mentioned in Alma chapter 52 and dates to 64 B.C. It's in these three places—Nephi, Zarahemla, and Bountiful—where there is mention of a temple. For the purposes of this section, we will focus solely on details the Book of Mormon gives about Bountiful.

The city of Bountiful is probably surrounded by the state or larger land of Bountiful, as are Nephi and Zarahemla surrounded by their respective larger lands, each bearing its corresponding name. The city Bountiful has its reference point in relation to the city of Mulek, which was located in the East Wilderness, in the borders by the seashore (see Alma 51:21–27). Inasmuch as Mulek was close to the city Bountiful, it was still part of Zarahemla since Moroni had annexed the East Wilderness a few years earlier (see Alma 46:17).

The above information, coupled with the evidence already presented which proposes the Mayan site of Cerros in northern Belize to be the city of Mulek, enables us to suggest a general area for the city Bountiful. Two major archaeological sites located in the Southern Yucatan Peninsula, Dzibanche and Kohunlich, are within a short distance of the proposed city of Mulek. Although we had been taking groups for years to the archaeological zone of Kohunlich, Dzibanche was only accessible to the public as recently as 1997. Dzibanche (pronounced *see-bahn-chey*) means "writing on wood." I first visited this site in February of 1997, shortly after its opening. Several details caught my attention and convinced me of a possible correlation between this ancient site and the city of Bountiful where the Savior visited the Nephites.

(1) There were newly planted, green stalks of corn growing alongside golden, eight-foot stalks ready to harvest, with intermediate sizes of corn growing in other fields nearby. My farmer's instinct caused me to wonder how this continual harvest could be possible, and I began to look around for irrigation water, a sprinkling system, or some other source of water. It wasn't until later that we discovered that the crops were watered by a gentle dew that fell on the ground each morning. This allowed for the crops to grow all year round, as opposed to being limited to the rainy season.

THE LAND BOUNTIFUL 65

(2) I was overwhelmed with the large number and immense size of the buildings. As we entered the city, we could still see the remains of the fortified earthworks embankment that had been constructed centuries earlier to protect the city. To get into what are several large plazas, visitors must ascend the remains of an ancient dirt embankment that surrounds the "city of wood." Of course, the wooden timbers on top of the embankment are gone, but the dirt ditch and its high inner embankment still remains. Like its neighbors Becan, Cerros, Calakmul, and Tikal—Dzibanche also contains remnants of defensive earthworks.

(3) The most impressive thing to me about Dzibanche is the multitude of peaceful groves surrounding the ruins, with ample room to walk between the towering trees. This is different from Tikal with its tall, dense jungle growth, and also different from Northern Yucatan with its thick scrub brush. The cool gentle breeze makes Dzibanche truly a "bountiful" setting.

THE GREAT DESTRUCTION

In 3 Nephi we read, "The whole face of the land was changed, because of the tempest and the whirlwinds, and the thunderings and the lightnings, and the exceeding great quaking of the whole earth" (3 Nephi 8:12).

When Hebrew-trained writer, Mormon, uses the phrases, "the whole face of the land" and "the whole earth," he is (1) outlining the great destruction at the time of Christ in poetic parallel sentences, and (2) he is explaining in Hebrew terms that "whole" means "that which was changed, was changed completely." We are not to infer that *every* mountain throughout Mesoamerica, or for that matter the entire universe, was completely transformed. However, for the ones that *were* changed, there was a complete alteration. In other words, all that quaked, quaked. That's "the learning of the Jews" for you.

Without taking into consideration a subsequent verse that states that the "earth did cleave together" (3 Ne. 10:10), some have used this verse in an attempt to prove that studying Book of Mormon geography isn't possible because the "whole face of the land was changed." This statement is flawed for two reasons:

Mormon wrote his history 300 years after the destruction and yet he could still identify the same sites that existed prior to the destruction. Hence, the land wasn't changed so dramatically that the places where they lived could not be located or recognized.

Not all places were destroyed. The city of Bountiful was spared, and Zarahemla was burned and then rebuilt. And those places which were destroyed are now showing up as described by the Book of Mormon itself. Chiutinamit, which was covered with water, Cholula, which was destroyed and then rebuilt, and Cuicuilco, which was covered with lava—each of these has since been discovered. Destructions actually preserve areas that can now be investigated, enabling us to examine ancient pottery styles, food consumption, and living conditions.

The oral and written history of Mesoamerica not only provides us with additional insights, but it also confirms the actuality of the destruction itself. Ixtlilxochitl placed the date of the destruction at the exact time given in the Book of Mormon (3 Ne. 8:5).[2]

Mesoamerica is certainly an adequate stage for the great destruction that occurred at the death of Christ. More than thirty volcanoes dot the landscape of Guatemala alone. From time to time they explode violently, covering villages and taking lives. Hardly a year goes by without a great earthquake being reported somewhere in Mexico or Central America.

Perhaps the greatest lesson we learn from this section of the Book of Mormon, however, is that the famines, wars, and the great destruction preceding the advent of Christ to the Nephites is a type and a shadow of His Second Coming, to which we look in our day. And just as the righteous were spared in that day, we too will find safety in these last days if we are prepared to receive Him.

THE PASSOVER AT BOUNTIFUL AND THE ADVENT OF CHRIST

The entire message of the Book of Mormon is brought to a climax with the words, "I am Jesus Christ, whom the prophets testified shall come into the world" (3 Ne. 11:10). And the depth of the feelings generated by those who had looked to His coming are captured in the words, "no one can conceive of the joy which filled our souls at the time we heard him pray for us unto the Father" (3 Ne. 17:17). This was that white God, spoken of for centuries later, whose "countenance did smile upon them [his disciples], and the light of his countenance did shine upon them, and behold they were as white as the countenance and also the garments of Jesus; and behold the whiteness thereof did exceed all the whiteness, yea, even there could be nothing upon earth so white as the whiteness thereof" (3 Ne. 19:25).

As Christ taught the Nephites at Bountiful, many marveled when He told them that "old things had passed away" (3 Ne. 15:2). By "old things," He meant the law of Moses had been fulfilled and that it was no longer necessary to follow, since the law was only there to prepare and point them to Christ.

> I am he that gave the law, and I am he who covenanted with my people Israel; therefore, the law in me is fulfilled, for I have come to fulfill the law; therefore it hath an end (3 Ne. 15:5).

This law that was given to Moses began in Egypt when the people were instructed to put lamb's blood on their doors, symbolic of the Lamb's blood on the cross. This was done in order that death—both spiritual and physical—would pass over those who would bow and confess that Jesus is the Christ. It was the Savior who gave the law to Moses, and in commemoration of what would become an infinite Atonement, a *Pass Over* was established in Israel. The Passover was brought to the promised land at 600 B.C., and a righteous segment of the population continued to look forward to the fulfillment of the law.

Christ was born, and crucified, at the time of the Passover; and from what we now know it appears that Lehi left Jerusalem at the time of the Passover, as well. From a Mesoamerican perspective, the signs of Christ's death and His appearance to the Nephites also occurred at the time of the Passover. According to Dr. Bruce Warren's work with Mayan calendar decipherment, Christ's death fell on Friday, April 1, A.D. 33 and His appearance to the Nephites took place on March 29, A.D. 34.[3]

Opposite and Above: Little children among the fortified ruins of Becán in southern Campeche. "Even if they should dwindle in unbelief, the Lord shall prolong their days . . . [and] they shall again be brought to the true knowledge" (Helaman 15:11, 13).

Mormon wrote that at the end of the thirty-fourth year, the Savior appeared to the Nephites (see 3 Ne. 10:18–19). However, the destruction which marked the death of Christ occurred at the beginning of the thirty-fourth year (see 3 Ne. 8:5). In other words, almost a year elapsed from the time of the destruction to the time that Christ arrived at Bountiful. Both dates appear to fall on Easter, or the time of the Passover.

We may wonder why the Savior appeared to the Nephites at Bountiful, when there was a temple in Zarahemla. A glyph engraved in stone at Chiapa de Corzo, located in the area proposed as Zarahemla, gives the date of December 7, 36 B.C. As mentioned earlier, this date may represent Lamanite occupation of the Central Depression area of Zarahemla (see Hel. 4:4–5). Correspondingly, verse 6 informs us that at that same time the Nephites and the armies of Moronihah were driven even into the land of Bountiful. We know this has reference to the city of Bountiful because of a statement we read in Helaman 5:14.

Hence, the headquarters of the Church moved to the city Bountiful about thirty-six years before Christ was born. That would explain why a temple was built at Bountiful and why the righteous Nephites were present at Bountiful instead of Zarahemla when Christ descended from heaven. From other Mesoamerican sources,

68 SACRED SITES

we are led to consider that Bountiful may not have been the only place the Savior visited during His sojourn among the Nephites. Ixtlilxochitl wrote that Quetzalcoatl lingered long in several places and that he taught his doctrine at Cholula, but with little success.[4]

QUETZALCOATL, THE WHITE GOD

As I was working on a higher degree at Brigham Young University in the discipline of Ancient and Modern Scripture, I became intrigued with statements that had surfaced over the years about a white god that figured prominently in the religious tradition of Mesoamerica. My trail took me to El Paso, Texas where I had been assigned to the institute of religion, and subsequently to Mexico City, where I had the opportunity to conduct research for a dissertation, which I entitled: *A comparative study of Quetzalcoatl, the Feathered-Serpent God of Meso-America, with Jesus Christ, the god of the Nephites.*[5]

From that experience, two things surfaced. (1) The legends and traditions of a god whose attributes seemed to resemble those of the Savior in minute detail were voluminous, and (2) the legends and traditions of a god whose attributes more resembled paganism, and whose time line does not correspond with the Savior's visit to the Nephites, were also abundant.

As one writer stated, "In all of America's past no figure is more exciting, more tantalizing, or more frustrating than that of the fair god Quetzalcoatl."[6] Even the name Quetzalcoatl presents considerable dilemma. *Quetzal* is associated with a bird with long beautiful tail feathers. *Coatl* is a Nauhtl (Aztec) word for "serpent." For that reason, Quetzalcoatl is often referred to as "the feathered-serpent god."

I do believe that the advent of Christ to the Nephites was of such magnitude that a tradition was established which became engraved in the hearts of people throughout Mesoamerica. As time elapsed, this tradition became polluted, as reflected in art, folklore, and written records.

The sixteenth-century Mexican writer Ixtlilxochitl wrote, "Quetzalcoatl was a man of comely appearance and serious disposition. His countenance was white, and he wore a beard. His manner of dress consisted of a long, flowing robe."[7]

Other similarities with Christ and Quetzalcoatl include a virgin birth, creator of all things, performer of miracles, prophesier of future events with a promise to return, teacher of the law of the fast, and the ordinance of baptism. A new star is also associated with both Christ and Quetzalcoatl, and symbols of death and resurrection are prominent in both of their histories.[8]

So what's the problem? The problem is that in Mexican folklore there was a tenth-century personage who has also been labeled the "white god Quetzalcoatl." He was born A.D. 935, took upon himself the name Quetzalcoatl, was driven out of the Mexico Valley, and resurfaced in the Yucatan area. Today at Chichen Itza there is a temple called Kukulcan, which is the Mayan word for "feathered serpent." Every year at the spring and fall equinox, the shadows caused by the setting of the sun are cast upon the backs of the sculpted serpents on the building, as though the serpent god is returning to earth. It is this pagan god that is sometimes mistaken as a representation of Christ.

We may also wonder if the name "Quetzalcoatl" poses a problem. The answer is no. It was Moses who lifted the brazen serpent upon the pole in similitude of Christ, who would be lifted up on the cross (see Num. 21:5; John 3:14–15). Similarly, Book of Mormon prophets also associated Christ with a serpent. (See Hel. 8:13–15; Alma 33:19.) To me, the symbolism is clear and profound. It is connected to the concept that Nephi struggled with when asked if he understood the condescension of God (see 1 Ne. 11:16). From His throne on high, God—even the Savior of the world—descended as low as the serpent as He walked the earth and suffered in both flesh and spirit. But He was and is God, and as such ascended to the heavens, as represented symbolically by that beautiful quetzal bird whose iridescent tail feathers capture the sunrays in its flight toward heaven. The serpent represents death, the quetzal represents the resurrection. The tragedy is that in Mesoamerican art the Quetzal-Coatl concept has been reduced to stone, just as in the world of Christianity, Christ is still left hanging on the cross.[9]

Opposite: "All the glory of the godhead, had the prophet Quetzalcoatl:
All the honor of the people, sanctified his name and holy;
And their prayers they offered to him in the days of ancient Tula" (Exploring the Lands of the Book of Mormon, 162).
Tula is translated as "Bountiful." Many Maya priests invoked the name of Quetzalcoatl, as indicated by the feathered headdress of the Quetzal bird shown here.

Above: Copy of a Maya Classic time period mural at the Holiday Inn in Chetumal, Quintana Roo, Mexico. Notice the quetzal feathers on the headdresses of the two overlords. You will also observe that the panel is written in a Hebrew chiasmic pattern of A-B-B-A. A-Overlord B-Slave B-Slave A-Overlord

CHAPTER SIX
THE LAND OF DESOLATION

The land on the northward was called Desolation. (Alma 22:31)

A SMALL NECK OF LAND

The definition of an isthmus is "a small neck of land connecting two larger land areas." The Book of Mormon defines it as a small neck of land that divided the land of Desolation or land northward from the land Bountiful or land southward (Alma 22:32). There is a strong agreement among Latter-day Saint scholars that the Isthmus of Tehuantepec in Mexico is that narrow neck of land spoken of in the Book of Mormon. There is also a narrow pass, as required by the Book of Mormon, which moves directly north to south from the Gulf of Tehuantepec to the Gulf of Mexico. The definition of a gulf is "a part of an ocean or sea extending into the land." The Gulf of Mexico is probably the area referred to as the "place where the sea divides the land" (Ether 10:20).

Most Book of Mormon history took place in the Land Southward; however, several significant events also occurred in the Land Northward. They include the landing places of both the Jaredites and the Mulekites, the Jaredites' land of first inheritance, the heartland of the Jaredites' history, the destination of Nephite migrations, and the place where both the Jaredite and Nephite nations came to a violent close.

The Hill Shim, as well as the Hill Ramah/Cumorah, is located in the Land Northward. The "land among many waters" (Mosiah 8:8) was located on the southward side of the Land Northward, and the waters of

Above: The land Northward was called the land Desolation by the Nephites because of the great civilization that had previously been destroyed there (Helaman 3:6).

Opposite: Monument representing an Olmec/Jaredite king holding a child in its arms. May suggest the anointing of a young king. Discovered at the site of La Venta, Tabasco, Mexico, and now located at the outdoor La Venta Museum in Villahermosa. La Venta has been proposed as the Jaredite city of Lib (Ether 10:19–20).

Ripliancum were located on the northward side and close to the Hill Ramah/Cumorah (Ether 15:8–11). The Land Northward was heavily populated and the Land Southward, where Zarahemla was located, was preserved as a wilderness to hunt wild animals for food (Ether 10:21).

Some of the prominent cities in the Land Northward include the city of Lib, the city of Kish, the city of Desolation, and the city of Teancum. The lands of Antum, Cumorah, Moron, and "the land which was northward" (probably the Mexico Valley) were all located in the Land Northward (Alma 50:29).

Some of the major personalities who lived in the Land Northward were all of the Jaredite kings, including Jared, Omer, Heth, Shiblom, Kish, Lib, Shiz, and Coriantumr. Three of the great authors of the Book of Mormon—Ether, Mormon, and Moroni—all lived in the Land Northward. Both Mormon and Moroni lived in the city of Desolation, which was near the narrow pass that led into the Land Southward (Morm. 3:5).

Three major Mesoamerican civilizations encompass areas in what would have been the Land Northward during the Nephite time period. They are the Zapotecs of the Valley of Oaxaca, the Teotihuacan culture of the Valley of Mexico, and the Olmec civilization with headquarters along the Gulf Coast of Mexico, which is the modern-day state of Veracruz.

Although a major portion of the Land Northward was called the land of Desolation, the area itself is not desolate. Indeed, the Gulf Coast is the "golden lane of Mexico." Its Hawaiian-type climate can grow anything, including pineapple, sugar cane, cacao, tobacco, rice, bananas, oranges, and virtually anything that is planted in the earth. It is a common sight to see trees that have been cut down to form fence posts, growing into trees again. Living in Utah, the opposite happens to me. It seems that every time I plant a tree, it turns into a post. Water is abundant in the Tuxtla mountain region, and Veracruz's reputation as the most beautiful state in Mexico is legendary.

Mormon informs us that no part of the land was desolate, save it were for timber. It is only because of the great destruction of the people who had before inhabited the land that this area was termed "desolate" (Hel. 3:6).

THE MULEKITES' LANDING SITE

We read in Alma 22:30 that the people of Zarahemla, whom we often call the Mulekites, landed among the Jaredite nation. Because of several statements in the Book of Mormon, accompanied with archaeological and historical evidence that locate the Jaredites along the Gulf of Mexico, we can determine that the Mulekites crossed the Atlantic Ocean and landed near Veracruz, Mexico. (See the following section.) Local Mexican history tells of nine ships (whose passengers were descendants of Abraham and Jacob), that landed at the Bay of Panuco, which is near the state of Veracruz, Mexico.[1] A portion of the Mulekites, or the people of Zarahemla, then migrated into the Land Southward to the place called Zarahemla, where Mosiah discovered them about 200 B.C. (Omni 1:13–14).

If the Mulekites left at the time of the Babylonian conquest of 586 B.C., then it is possible that they would have arrived in the promised land as early as 585 B.C. Had they waited until after the Jews' release from bondage fifty-two years later, the date of 533 is more practical. This later date more closely fits the pattern developed by Cyrus Gordon in relation to the discovery of the Paraiba stone in Brazil, whose engravings seem to speak of this same voyage.[2] This may answer why Mulek was not killed by the Babylonians when they killed all of the other sons of Zedekiah. He was not yet born. The fact that Zedekiah was only thirty-two years old at the time certainly allows for him to have had other children while in bondage.

A LAND AMONG MANY WATERS

We read in Mosiah 8 that the puppet King Limhi, who was living with a colony of Nephites in the land of Nephi, desired to get out of bondage from the Lamanites. He therefore sent an expedition of forty-three men to go down to Zarahemla and appeal to his brethren to deliver them out of bondage. Three generations had elapsed from the time that Mosiah had gone down to Zarahemla, or a total of about eighty years. The distance from Nephi to Zarahemla was about 250 miles.[3]

THE LAND DESOLATION 73

Top: The Olmec civilization, whose heartland was in the Gulf Coast area of Mexico, is considered the mother civilization of the Americas. These Olmec heads are representative of over 30 Olmec stone heads that have been discovered in the Gulf Coast region of Mexico. The Olmec history, as represented in its art, is comparable to the Jaredite history recorded in Ether and is literally a story of kingship.

Bottom: These mosaics are representative of a serpent and are located at the outdoor La Venta Park in Villahermosa. Originally discovered at the site of La Venta, Tabasco, Mexico, and was buried 20 feet below the surface. May symbolically represent the overthrow of secret combinations in the 10th century B.C. among the Jaredites. (Ether 10:19)

Above: Lake Catemaco is located about 30 miles east of the Hill Vigia and as such is considered by many Latter-day Saint scholars to be part of the land of Cumorah which was a land of "many waters, rivers and fountains." (Mormon 6:4)

Not knowing the trail, and because of the ruggedness of the terrain, it would have been a difficult trip. They may have known the distance and they may have been told that the river ran through Zarahemla. My guess is that once they had arrived to the Cuchumatanes mountain range, where the waters travel north, they got off on the wrong tributary. Had they followed the Grijalva River, they would have run into Zarahemla.[4] However, had they mistakenly followed the Usumacinta River, they would have not found any cities of consequence at 121 B.C. The flow of the river would have taken them directly into "a land among many waters," or the vast lagoon systems between the states of Campeche and Tabasco, Mexico.

However, they did find the ruins of the ancient Jaredites, including twenty-four gold plates, which told their ancient history. An abridgement of that history is included in the Book of Mormon and is called the book of Ether.

The Hagoth Shipping Lane

For more than eleven years, from 56 B.C. to 45 B.C., shipping took place from the Land Southward to the Land Northward, which is as near as can be determined today from the Gulf of Tehuantepec to the Bay of Acapulco. The geographical description reports that Hagoth built the ships "on the borders of the land Bountiful, by the land Desolation, and launched it forth into the west sea, by the narrow neck of land which led into the land northward" (Alma 63:5). The inland trail from Acapulco to the ancient trade route site of Xochicalco, and then on into the Mexico Valley, would have been much more efficient than traveling by land through the Isthmus of Tehuantepec (narrow pass) on into Veracruz, and subsequently into the Mexico Valley.

Along with people, one of the more common items being shipped was timber, due to a lack of it in the Land Northward. To this day there is a wealth of timber in the Gulf of Tehuantepec region, whereas it is virtually nonexistent in Mexico City. Most of the homes today in the Mexico Valley are still built of cement. "The people who went forth [into the land which was northward] became exceedingly expert in the working of cement; therefore they did build houses of cement, in the which they did dwell" (Hel. 3:7).

THE LAND DESOLATION 75

THE A.D. 350 TREATY

There is a treaty mentioned in Mormon 2:28–29 that is actually between three parties—the Lamanites, the Nephites, and the Gadianton robbers.

> In the three hundred and fiftieth year we made a treaty with the Lamanites and the robbers of Gadianton, in which we did get the land of our inheritance divided. And the Lamanites did give unto us the land northward, yea, even to the narrow passage which led into the land southward. And we did give unto the Lamanites all the land southward.

David Palmer, author of *In Search of Cumorah,* proposed that the Gadianton robbers probably had their headquarters in the Mexico Valley. That hypothesis now has excellent archaeological support. Archaeologist David Stuart of Harvard has shown a connection between Teotihuacan and Tikal in the fourth century A.D.[5]

The concept is that Mexico (Gadianton robbers) and the Mayan world (Lamanites in the Land Southward) wanted to establish trade relations. The Nephites, the third party to the treaty, were in the middle. The simple solution was to get rid of them. Mormon said they had the land of their inheritance divided and they were exiled from Zarahemla and forced to move to the other side of the isthmus where the city and land of Desolation was located. This explains why the Nephites were living in the ancient Jaredite territory at the time of their A.D. 385 battle with the Lamanites (Morm. 4–6).

THE HILL SHIM

Both Mormon and Moroni lived in the Land Northward. We know this from the following statements:

<u>MORMON:</u> (1) "I, being eleven years old, was carried by my father into the land southward, even to the land of Zarahemla" (Morm. 1:6), and (2) "I did cause my people that they should gather themselves together at the land Desolation, to a city which was in the borders, by the narrow pass which led into the land southward" (Morm. 3:5).

<u>MORONI:</u> (1) "I, Moroni, proceed to give an account of those ancient inhabitants who were destroyed by the hand of the Lord upon the face of this north country" (Ether 1:1), and (2) "After the great and tremendous battle at Cumorah, behold, the Nephites who had escaped into the country southward" (Morm. 8:2).

Inasmuch as both Mormon and Moroni lived in the Land Northward and also close to the narrow pass that led into the Land Southward, then the Hill Shim was also in the Land Northward, close to the narrow neck of land. It was also close to the seashore and the Hill Cumorah. It is the Hill Shim, however, that would be considered as Mormon's library. He was instructed by Ammoron to go to this hill and to *only* take the plates of Nephi and write a history of his people, leaving the rest of the records there. At the age of twenty-four, Mormon did that which he was instructed to do and abridged what today is called the Book of Mormon. The remainder of the records would stay in the Hill Shim for another forty years, at which time Mormon moved them from the Hill Shim to the Hill Cumorah (Morm. 4:23).

This Olmec figure with a corn headdress may suggest his name. The word for corn in Maya is X-im pronounced in English as Shim. Shim is both a Mayan and a Book of Mormon word. (Mormon 1:3; 4:23; Ether 9:3)

76 SACRED SITES

Above: Looking out from the top of Hill Vigia (Lookout Hill) located in the Tuxtla Mountain range in the state of Veracruz, Mexico is the proposed location of the Hill Ramah/Cumorah where the decisive battles of both the Jaredites and Nephites took place as well as the hiding place for all of the records that Mormon hid up in the Hill Cumorah with the exception of the plates which he gave his son, Moroni, from which the Book of Mormon was taken. (Mormon 6:6) "And it came to pass that the army of Coriantumr did pitch their tents by the Hill Ramah; and it was the same hill where my father Mormon did hide up the records unto the Lord, which were sacred" (Ether 15:11). "O ye fair sons and daughters, ye fathers and mothers, ye husbands and wives, ye fair ones, how is it that ye could have fallen!" (Mormon 6:19).

Inset: "Omer . . . came over and passed by the hill of Shim, and came over by the place where the Nephites were destroyed." (Ether 9:3) The hill shown here is called Cin in the Nahuatl (Aztec) language or X-im in the Maya language (pronounced Shim) and means corn in both languages. It is also the place where Mormon received the records from Ammoron. (Mormon 1:3; 2:17)

THE LAND DESOLATION

And now, I, Mormon, seeing that the Lamanites were about to overthrow the land, therefore I did go to the hill Shim, and did take up all the records which Ammoron had hid up unto the Lord (Morm. 4:23).

There is a hill in the state of Veracruz, Mexico, and close to the Isthmus of Tehuantepec, which today carries the same name as the Hill Shim. It is recorded in the Nauhtl or Aztec language as *Cin Tepec*, which means, "corn hill." The Mayan word for "corn" is *shim*, the name of the hill where the records entrusted to Mormon were located.

THE HILL RAMAH/CUMORAH

As the Nephite nation was primed for destruction Mormon wrote:

I made this record out of the plates of Nephi, and hid up in the hill Cumorah all the records which had been entrusted to me by the hand of the Lord, save it were *these few plates* which I gave unto my son Moroni (Morm. 6:6; emphasis added).

The Hill Ramah of the Jaredites was the same hill as the Hill Cumorah of the Nephites (Ether 15:11), and the Hill Shim is located nearby (Morm. 1:3; 4:23). Correspondingly, there is a hill located in the Tuxtla mountain region and close to the Hill Shim, which is called Vigia, or "lookout hill." It is this hill that was proposed by David Palmer as the Hill Ramah/Cumorah of the Book of Mormon. He wrote, "I will not prove definitively that it is the correct place. However, there is strong archaeological evidence. Any other candidate would have to pass through the same strainer of criteria to which we subject the cerro Vigia."[6]

Mormon transferred the records from the Hill Shim to the Hill Ramah/Cumorah. A short time later, he gave his son Moroni "these few plates," and it is "these few plates" that Moroni carried to New York and buried in a hill near Palmyra, which plates Joseph Smith unearthed and translated 1400 years later. Most of the records, however, Mormon left buried in the Hill Cumorah (Morm. 6:6). Moroni wrote that he would also "write and hide up the records in the earth," that is, the record his father gave him—or the Book of Mormon (Morm 8:4). Moroni left the Land of Desolation area to travel to New York sometime after A.D. 400. His last entry in the Book of Mormon was A.D. 421 (Moro. 1:3).

I believe that the Hill Cumorah where Mormon deposited "all the records" is different from the hill where Joseph Smith retrieved the plates that Moroni had "hid up in the earth." In my opinion, the only place where the Hill Cumorah of the Book of Mormon *cannot* be is in New York where the Prophet Joseph Smith received "those few plates" that Mormon gave to his son Moroni. I have come to this conclusion largely because of the countless Mesoamerican parallels, many of which are presented in this book.

THE WATERS OF RIPLIANCUM

Like the Hill Shim, a large body of water has also been discovered that carries the same meaning as Ripliancum—that is, "exceeding large waters." The name in the Aztec language is *Hueyapan* and it is located near the Hill Vigia, a leading candidate for the Hill Ramah/Cumorah.

Today, this massive water basin is called Papaoloapan, which means "butterfly" because it drains out of the mountains of Puebla and Veracruz and spreads out like a butterfly, creating a large water basin. It then drains into the Gulf of Mexico, forming a water barrier that fits into the geographical description in the Book of Mormon.[7]

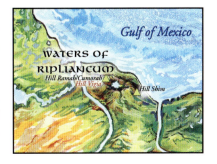

IN THE MOUTH OF TWO OR THREE WITNESSES

Three separate, yet parallel accounts help to give us a fuller understanding of the mother civilization of the Americas. They are the book of Ether and the account of the Jaredites, the archaeological record and the account of the Olmecs, and the record of Ixtlilxochitl and the account of the first settlers.

THE BOOK OF MORMON RECORD (JAREDITES)	1) <u>The First Civilization</u>: According to his memory, Moroni wrote an account of "those ancient inhabitants." In other words, he wrote a brief history of the oldest civilization referred to in the Book of Mormon. They are called the Jaredites, named after their first king, Jared (Ether 1:1, 33; 5:1; Moro. 9:23–24).	2) <u>The Great Tower and the Pacific Route</u>: The Jaredites came from the tower of Babel at the time of the confusion of tongues, and yet the Lord did not confound their own. As near as can be determined, their route of travel brought them through China across the Pacific Ocean, where they were on the water for 344 days. "No monster of the sea could break them, neither whale that could mar them" (Ether 6:10–11).[8]	3) <u>Headquarters in the Land Northward</u>: According to Moroni the Jaredites lived upon the "face of this north country," or the Land Northward. The city of Desolation was located in the "borders by the narrow pass which led into the land southward" (Morm. 3:5).
THE ARCHAEOLOGICAL RECORD (OLMECS)	(1) <u>The First Civilization</u>: According to the archaeological record, the Olmecs are "the mother civilization of the Americas." Their history is engraved on stones, and their remains have been discovered under mounds of dirt. The word *Olmec* means "rubber tree," referring to the area where the ancient Olmecs had their heartland. The Olmecs were not considered to be the first civilization of the Americas until an ancient date glyph, discovered by Matthew Stirling, was reported in a conference in Mexico on July 7, 1941.[9]	2) <u>The Great Tower and the Pacific Route</u>: While there is not enough evidence at this time to support that the Olmecs originated from the tower of Babel, there is an engraved stone located at the outdoor La Venta museum that supports an ocean crossing and the concept that "no monster of the sea" could destroy them. The engraved monuments and calendar structure also manifest a direct tie to China, which would suggest a Pacific crossing.[10]	3) <u>Headquarters in the Land Northward</u>: The homeland of the ancient Olmecs is centered along the Gulf of Mexico, where between 1500 and 400 B.C., they developed a massive civilization. The gulf coast region is referred to as "northern parts of the land," with the Gulf of Tehuantepec as the point of reference. The Olmec lands of Veracruz, Tabasco, Oaxaca, Puebla, and Tampico are northward of the Isthmus of Tehuantepec. When the great storms come off the coast of Veracruz today, they are referred to as *los nortes*, or the "northern winds."
THE HISTORICAL RECORD (16TH CENTURY HISTORIAN)	1) <u>The First Civilization</u>: Don Fernando de Alba de Ixtlilxochitl was a mixture of Spanish and Toltec royalty. He grew up in Texcoco, a suburb of Mexico City. He gained a great deal of fame as a court recorder and as author of "a history of the events in New Spain (Mexico)," which was written in Spanish and published in 1600. He referred to the mother civilization as the first settlers to occupy the land of New Spain. He reported that he obtained his information about the first civilization of Mesoamerica from the ancient histories and from the oral traditions.[12]	2) <u>The Great Tower and the Pacific Route</u>: Ixtlilxochitl reported that after the Flood, the people of the earth began again to populate the earth. They built a high tower to protect them from a second destruction and "their language became confounded, such that they did not understand one another and they were scattered to all parts of the world."[13] Ixtlilxochitl continues; "The Tultecas [referring to the first settlers], consisting of seven men and their wives were able to understand one another, and they came to this land having crossed many lands and waters, living in caves and passing through great tribulations. Upon their arrival here, they discovered that it was a very good and fertile land."[14] That they crossed the Pacific Ocean is consistent with Jaredite and Olmec history. Ixtlilxochitl wrote, "They came from the great Tartary [China] and were part of those who came from the division of Babel."[15]	3) <u>Headquarters in the Land Northward</u>: Ixtlilxochitl reports that the first settlers or the mother civilization of Mesoamerica "populated the major part of the land and more particularly that which fall among the northern part."[16] This referring to the area along the Gulf of Mexico and is consistent with the geographical location of the Jaredites and the Olmecs. 

THE LAND DESOLATION 79

In conclusion, the individual testimonies of the Jaredites, Olmecs, and the Chichimecatleach each combine to place the mother civilization of the Americas along the Gulf of Mexico. This sets the stage for the final geographical backdrop in the Book of Mormon—the great Lamanite-Nephite battle of A.D. 385 (Morm. 6:2–15).

A High Civilization	5) A Large People	6) Nation Destroyed by Civil War	7) Deity Associated with a Serpent
A High Civilization: The Jaredites were "as numerous as the hosts of Israel" as determined by their remains, including their many buildings (Mosiah 8:8). Indeed, the whole face of the land northward was covered with inhabitants" (Ether 10:21). For over thirty generations they were governed by kings. They kept a written record (Mosiah 8:9).	5) A Large People: Moroni called the brother of Jared a "large and mighty man" (Ether 1:34), and at the end of the record, he records that the Jaredites were "large and mighty men as to the strength of men" (Ether 15:26). The forty-three-man search party, sent from the land of Nephi, apparently tried on the breastplates of the Jaredites and reported that they were very large (Mosiah 8:10).	6) Nation Destroyed by Civil War: Ether describes in vivid detail the final and decisive battle between Coriantumr and Shiz (Ether 15:29–31). Previously, the record reported that over two million "mighty men, and also their wives and their children" had been destroyed (Ether 15:2). This does not mean that every last man, woman, and child was killed. It means the Jaredite nation fell. As was prophesied by Ether, eventually Coriantumr and all his household (heirs to the throne) were killed (Ether 13:20–21). As near as can be determined from internal evidence in the Book of Mormon, the Jaredite nation fell between 300–200 B.C.	7) Deity Associated with a Serpent: The serpent motif is associated in the scriptures—including the Book of Mormon—with Christ, who would be lifted up that man might live. (See Alma 53:19; Hel. 8:13–15.) Old Testament prophets testified of the reality of Christ and His mission, as did Book of Mormon prophets, including the brother of Jared.
A High Civilization: The Olmecs supported a kingship hierarchy, a detail gathered from studying over thirty large stone heads that have been discovered in the region. Although the language has not yet been deciphered, the evidence of a written language and a consistent calendar system are recognizable. No other area in all of the Americas reached the stature and population size to qualify as a high civilization in that time period. It is for the above reasons that the Olmecs are represented as the mother civilization of Mesoamerica.	5) A Large People: The Olmecs, as determined by their artwork and their monuments, were a large people. Their descendants still exist today with that same profile. Their physical profiles appear to be closely related to some of the Polynesian cultures with which we are familiar.	6) Nation Destroyed by Civil War: In the 1960s, Michael Coe, one of the leading figures in Mesoamerican archaeology and a professor Emeritus from Yale University, conducted excavation and restoration work at the archaeological zone of La Venta. He reported that their destruction came about as the result of a massive civil war and that "its fall was certainly violent, as twenty-four of the forty sculptured monuments were intentionally mutilated."[11] A monument representing a king named Kix (Kish), as determined by deciphered glyphs at Palenque, manifests a body with the head and arms completely severed. This was discovered at the archaeological site of San Lorenzo.	7) Deity Associated with a Serpent: Kish is the name of both a Jaredite and an Olmec king. Chan Baalam, the son of Pacal of Palenque, traced his genealogy to an Olmec king named "U Kix Chan," who was born March 8, 993 B.C. The appendage to the name "Kix" (Kish) is associated with the serpent deity.
A High Civilization: Ixtlilxochitl affirms that they were a people who wrote their history and "according to what appears in their histories and paintings, they only made an abridgement, primarily of their origins." Their first king was named Chichimecatl. He brought them to "this new land where they settled and all who are now called Ultecas, Aculhuas, and Mexicanas, as well as the other people in the land, boast and affirm that they are descendants of the Chichimecas."[17] Although the names differ, the history is the same. The high civilization of the Jaredites, Olmecs, and the Chichimecas are likely talking about the same people.	5) A Large People: Ixtlilxochitl calls the native people of Mexico "giants," and these giants descended from the same Chichimecas mentioned earlier.[18] Again, this is consistent with the description given about the Jaredites and the Olmecs.	6) Nation Destroyed by Civil War: Ixtlilxochitl records that their "civilization came to an end as a result of great calamities and punishments from heaven."[19] By deduction of the dates provided by Ixtlilxochitl, they were destroyed at 249 B.C. This is consistent (give or take fifty years) with dates reported of both the Jaredite and Olmec destruction.	7) Deity Associated with a Serpent: The major deity mentioned by Ixtlilxochitl is Quetzalcoatl, and his dates correspond with the Book of Mormon date of Christ's death and the great destruction.[20] *Coatl* means "serpent" and reflects the same concept as identified in both the Jaredite and Olmec histories.

Bananas, pineapple, coconut and all kinds of fruits are grown along the Gulf of Mexico, homeland to the ancient Olmecs/Jaredites. This area is referred to as the Golden Lane of Mexico because of its plentiful harvests. It is also the heartland of the ancient Olmec/Jaredite civilization.

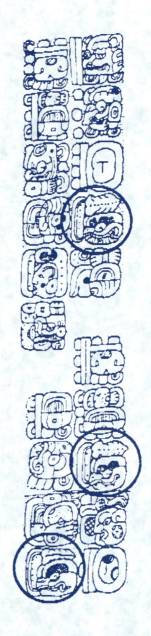

Above: This ancient, man-made pyramid dates to 1000 B.C. and is located at La Venta, Tabasco, near the Gulf of Mexico. It may have been the great city which Lib built "by the narrow neck of land, by the place where the sea divides the land" (Ether 10:20).

Upon observing the translation of the above glyphs from the Temple of the Cross at Palenque, Dr. Bruce Warren, an LDS archaeologist, discovered the name and birth date of a Jaredite king named Kish (glyph indicating his name is circled).

An artistic rendition by Cliff Dunston of Monument #47 at San Lorenzo, Tenochtitlan (located near the Gulf of Mexico)—a king whose name is deciphered as K'ix or Kish. Upon further investigation, Dr. Warren concluded that the monument shown here is the King Kish referred to in Ether 10:19, and was born on March 8, 993 B.C. His full name is U Kish Can and is associated with the feathered serpent.

The monument is three feet, three inches tall (without the head). The destruction of the monument occurred around 300 B.C., concurrent with the demise of the Jaredite civilization as a result of massive civil war.

CHAPTER SEVEN
MONTE ALBÁN

The people of Zarahemla and the people of Mosiah did unite together. (Omni 1:19)

THE OAXACA VALLEY

I believe that the Oaxaca Valley played a vital role in the development of the civilizations in the Book of Mormon. The area may have been the land of Moron in the early Jaredite/Olmec history. After the arrival of the Mulekites, the Oaxaca Valley may have become one of the areas where a branch of their society made its home. Certain sites, such as Monte Alban, give hints of their being under Nephite control beginning about 180 B.C.

The Zapotec civilization had its beginnings in the Valley of Oaxaca about 500 B.C. As determined by cultural patterns, language, and date correlations, the early Zapotecs may have been part of the Mulekite culture. The people of Zarahemla, who were Mulekites, merged with a group of Nephites led by King Mosiah about 200 B.C. (Omni 1:19).

The Oaxaca Valley is located northwest of the Isthmus of Tehuantepec. If the Isthmus of Tehuantepec is synonymous with the narrow neck of land in the Book of Mormon, then the Valley of Oaxaca was in the Land Northward. The land of Moron "was near the land which is called Desolation by the Nephites" (Ether 7:6). The ruins of San Jose Magote in the northern Oaxaca Valley date to the early Jaredite

Above: The state of Oaxaca is home to one of the largest indigenous populations of Mexico. The people known today as the Zapotecs, or people of the clouds, lived in the valley during the time period of the Book of Mormon and beyond. Some scholars propose the Oaxaca Valley to be the ancient Jaredite Land of Moron (see Ether 7:6).

Opposite: Located in the Oaxaca valley and built on a high hill, the ancient city of Monte Albán existed from 500 B.C.–A.D. 700. It may have been occupied by a remnant of the Mulekites as early as 500 B.C. and controlled by the Nephites beginning at the reign of King Mosiah at about 100 B.C. This spearhead with an Olmec face carved in it comes from Oaxaca and suggests early Jaredite occupation in the area around Monte Albán.

84 SACRED SITES

time period. According to Mexican archaeologist Ignacio Bernal, remains from that building show a style of brick similar to "far off Mesopotamia."[1] That is the area of the ancient tower of Babel and the original homeland of the Jaredites. This suggests that the Oaxaca Valley may have been the Jaredites' land of first inheritance. In fact, an abundance of ancient artifacts from the Oaxaca Valley show strong Olmec characteristics.

The early excavation work in Monte Albán was accomplished under the able direction of the Mexican archaeologist, Alfonso Caso, with the major portion of the excavations completed in the 1930s. Caso's magnificent discovery of Tomb 7 proclaimed the richness of culture among the ancient Zapotec people because of the tomb's cache of gold, turquoise, and jade. Maintenance and excavation work of these archaeological sites in the state of Oaxaca still continues today under the direction of the Mexican government.

MONTE ALBÁN PERIOD I: 500–100 B.C.

In addition to the Olmec structure and the Jaredite time period, another group of people appeared in the area around 500 B.C. The archaeological site of Monte Albán may have been home to a branch of the Mulekite culture. Several items have been discovered in the area, including a horned incense burner indigenous to Jewish worship, discovery of Hebrew words, and other historical, geographical, and artistic comparisons. There may even be a possible correlation between the "dancers" at Monte Albán, as representative of the Jewish captivity of 586 B.C.[2]

Above: The so-called dancer depicted in this jade carving appears to be representative of a captivity scene as the various monuments at Monte Albán show the figures without clothing and in suffering positions, which gives a hint of a possible correlation with the Jewish captivity by Babylon.

Opposite Top: A building from a later period covers a 500 B.C. structure at Monte Albán. The monuments in front are commonly referred to as the dancers and also date to 500 B.C.

Opposite Left: Evidence of writing in Mesoamerica was first discovered at Monte Albán and is different from the Maya writing. Evidence of the Hebrew language has been detected at the town of Zachilla located at the base of Monte Albán.

Opposite Center: Excavated in the 1930s under the leadership of Alfonso Caso, much of Monte Albán has been restored. The building in the foreground is labeled an observatory and dates to the time of Christ.

Opposite Right: At the downfall of Monte Albán in the 8th century A.D., the headquarters of the Zapotec Indians moved to Mitla, which continued to exist until the time of the Spanish conquest. Notice the intricate individual stone in the columns in the ruins at Mitla in the photo shown here.

MONTE ALBÁN 85

MONTE ALBÁN PERIOD II: 180 B.C.–A.D. 200

The archaeological record states that other people entered the Valley of Oaxaca between 200 and 100 B.C. They may have originated in Guatemala. At any rate, they brought with them a number of culture traits which mingled with those of the earlier period. This new culture has been entitled Monte Albán II. The period lasted roughly until the beginning of the Christian era, and the bearers of this culture only settled in a few places in the valleys. This suggests that they were a small group of conquerors who imposed their power over the earlier inhabitants. Because they did not disappear, we may assume that the two groups probably mingled over the course of time.³

This is consistent with the Book of Mormon record. Around 200 B.C., Mosiah led a righteous group of people from the land of Nephi down to the land of Zarahemla. Mosiah represented a minority group who "imposed their power," as Mosiah was made king over the earlier group, or the people of Zarahemla. The two groups did mingle in the course of time. The land of Zarahemla was located in the Land Southward and Monte Albán, Oaxaca, is located in the Land Northward. The Lord, through Ether, told Coriantumr that his kingdom would be given to another people (Ether 13:20–20). Oaxaca was part of the Jaredite kingdom. It appears that after the death of Coriantumr, Mosiah was not only king over the Mulekites in the Land Southward, but would have been accepted as king by other Mulekites throughout that land and perhaps even some leaderless Jaredites who lived in the Land Northward. Monte Albán may have been a city in the Land Northward controlled by King Mosiah.

MONTE ALBÁN PERIOD III: A.D. 200–350

During the years between A.D. 200 and 350, the following activities are reported, as deduced from the archaeological records of Monte Albán:

1) The Christian Influence. By A.D. 200, the stepped-fret decoration, representing a serpent called xicalcoliuhqui, was a frequent motif and was to become very popular.⁴ The origin of the serpent motif may be attributed to the coming of Christ to the Nephites.⁵

2) A Massive Building Program. Beginning about A.D. 200, a change in architectural style appeared at Monte Albán. In contrast with the former structures that were built out of enormous stones, buildings of this era were constructed out of small, well-cut stones. Virtually all of the buildings of Monte Albán postdate the A.D. 200 era. The buildings were decorated, and, as near as can be determined, many were painted red.⁶ This is the same time that false prophets and a massive building program began in the Book of Mormon (4 Ne. 1:24–49).

3) Priest Control. Parallel with what we read in the Book of Mormon, the controlling factions during

the A.D. 200–350 period were the priests. Special places were apparently built where the dignitaries could observe the ball games, and the tombs of the priests became more important and spacious (4 Ne. 1:24–49)[7]

4). False Gods. The Book of Mormon speaks of much wickedness, and departure from the true religion. During this time period, the vast increase in the number of gods that were worshiped by the people is extremely noticeable (4 Ne. 1:24–49).[8]

5) Trade Activity. Beginning at A.D. 300, as recorded in the Book of Mormon, the people grew rich in silver and gold and trafficked with one another (4 Ne. 1:46). During this time period, trade activity at Monte Albán began from the north with Teotihuacan in the Valley of Mexico, not from the south as before.[9]

MONTE ALBÁN PERIOD IV: A.D. 350–750

By A.D. 350, Monte Albán appears to have reached its height in terms of population. Indeed, shortly after A.D. 350, Monte Albán experienced a serious decline in population. This decline corresponds with the same time period when Mormon was calling the Nephites together to battle with the Lamanites. It also corresponds to the time period when the Nephites lost a major portion of their territory (Morm. 2:28–29). Finally, it was this same time period, A.D. 385, when the Nephites were destroyed as an entire nation (Morm. 6:2–16).[10]

Opposite: Jade figure with vase attached to back of head. Olmecs in Oaxaca predated the Monte Albán period and as a result, this area may have been the land of Moron, where the Jaredites originally settled. (Ether 7:6)

Left Top: The native people, descendants of the Zapotecs, continue the ancient traditions of their forefathers. Here, Doña Sofia in the town of Coyotepec in the Oaxaca valley continues the art of making black pottery.

Left Bottom: Monte (mount) Albán (white flower) is situated on the top of the hill in the Oaxaca valley. This model, located in the National Museum of Anthropology of Mexico, is an artistic representation of Monte Albán at the time the Nephite history came to an end.

BEFORE THERE WAS LIGHT
BEFORE THERE WAS DAY,
WHEN THERE WAS STILL DARKNESS,
THE GODS MET IN COUNCIL AT TEOTIHUACAN
— FLORENTINE CODEX —

chapter eight
TEOTIHUACAN

Jacob . . . commanded his people that they should take their flight into the northernmost part of the land, and there build up unto themselves a kingdom. (3 Nephi 7:12)

TEOTIHUACAN, THE CITY OF THE GODS

I believe that the early part of the Teotihuacan history included activities associated with Nephite migrations in the first century B.C. With evidence that has surfaced in the last few years, it now appears that Teotihuacan also played a major role in the downfall of the Nephite nation.

Teotihuacan, which means "the city of the gods" or "the place where men became gods," is about a forty-five minute drive northeast from Mexico City. Today, a community by the same name dwells near the ancient ruins. Oftentimes, the ruins are simply referred to as "the pyramids." The Pyramids of the Sun and of the Moon are the most imposing structures at Teotihuacan.

Since the fall of Teotihuacan, the Valley of Mexico, where present-day Mexico City is located, has continued to remain the homeland for many other major governments, including the A.D. 900–1200 Toltecs, the A.D. 1325–1521 Aztecs, and the A.D. 1521–1821 Spanish occupation.

Above: Map showing location of Teotihuacan. The Mexico Valley is often referred to as the Alta Plano of Mexcio. At the time of the Spanish conquest in the year 1521, the valley consisted of three large lakes and the Aztecs were the ruling power, and had been since A.D. 1325.

Opposite: Pyramid of the Sun. During Book of Mormon times the large city of Teotihuacan (300 B.C.–A.D. 750) was in existence. The Pyramid of the Sun shown here dates to the first century B.C., the same time people migrated from the land Southward and "became exceedingly expert in the working of cement" (Hel 3:7). The name "Teotihuacan" means, "the place of the gods," or "the place where men became gods."

TEOTIHUACAN PERIOD I: 50 B.C.–A.D. 200

The traditional history of Teotihuacan reports that "before there was light, before there was day, when there was still darkness, the gods met in council in Teotihuacan."[1]

A few years prior to the Christian era, the phase referred to as Teotihuacan Period I was initiated. During this 350-year time period, the city expanded to occupy more than twelve square miles; and the population grew to an estimated 25,000 to 30,000 people. The increase in population of Teotihuacan during Period I was caused largely by people who migrated to the Mexico Valley and then settled in the city of Teotihuacan.

A significant amount of construction took place during Period I of Teotihuacan. The main avenue, called the Avenue of the Dead, was completed and functional during this period. The Temple of the Sun was built during Period I virtually as it stands today. And the inner structure of the Temple of the Moon was also built during Period I. These buildings are contemporaries with the great pyramid of Cholula, which is located on the other side of the two volcanic mountain peaks, Popocatepetl and Ixtachihuatl.

It is during the Teotihuacan I Period that we witness the greatest activity between the Land Southward and the Land Northward. At the time of the building of the Pyramid of the Sun, we witness the greatest activity in the Book of Mormon. The history recorded in the books of Mosiah, Alma, Helaman, 3 Nephi, and 4 Nephi all took place during Period I of Teotihuacan.

Also during this time period (55 B.C.), a large company of Nephites migrated into "the land which was northward"—that is, the land that was northward from the land of Zarahemla. If the land of Zarahemla was located in what is today Chiapas, Mexico, near the Isthmus of Tehuantepec, then perhaps this migration ended up in the Mexico Valley. Mexico City is a land that is northward; in fact, Teotihuacan manifested an increase in population during this time period as a result of migrations from the southern areas. The shipping industry that was started by that "exceedingly curious man" Hagoth, who built "an exceedingly large ship," endured for several years (Alma 63:4–5). That shipping route appears to have followed the shoreline from the Isthmus of Tehuantepec to the bay of Acapulco and then inland to the Valley of Mexico.[2]

It was also during the period of Teotihuacan I that the wicked ruler Jacob became a king over the secret combination band that fled out of the Land Southward and went into the "northernmost part of the land" to build a kingdom. This was about 30 B.C. (3 Ne. 7:9–13). Sixty-four years later, "the great city of Jacobugath, which was inhabited by the people of king Jacob," was destroyed by fire (3 Ne. 9:9).

TEOTIHUACAN PERIOD II: A.D. 200–350

From A.D. 200 to 750, the ceremonial center of Quetzalcoatl flourished at Teotihuacan. During the 150 years called Teotihuacan Period II, the population of the city doubled in size, reaching an estimated 50,000 inhabitants. This increase occurred throughout Mesoamerica, and this era became known as the Classic period. This period corresponds with the period of apostasy in the Book of Mormon, which began at A.D. 200 (4 Ne. 1:24–49).[3] Teotihuacan itself became a significant pagan center, as represented in their paintings and their depictions on the stone monuments of Tlaloc and Quetzalcoatl, symbols of rain and sun.

The Pyramid of the Moon was completed during this period, as well as many other sizeable buildings. The most sensational structure built during Period II is the Temple of Quetzalcoatl. This temple is considered to be one of the major architectural accomplishments of the Teotihuacanos.

Cement was introduced into the Mexico Valley as early as the first century B.C., and it appears that it was this valley referred to in Helaman where they "became exceedingly expert in the working of cement, therefore they did build many houses of cement" (Hel. 3:9). The same is true today in the Mexico Valley. Most buildings are built out of cement.

Cement was utilized extensively in the construction of the buildings at Teotihuacan to hold lava rocks in place and to construct roadways and floors. Plaster covered the buildings, which were then painted in brilliant colors, typical of the colors that are found in the simple home dwellings in Mexico today. Murals and frescoes, which are also reminiscent of the manner in which the Mexican culture is portrayed today, graced the walls of the buildings of Teotihuacan during Period II.

TEOTIHUACAN PERIOD III: A.D. 350–600

The population reached a high of about 200,000 inhabitants, which probably made Teotihuacan the largest city of the world during this 250-year time period. Today, Mexico City, with over 26 million people, shares this same fame of being the largest city in the world.

Teotihuacan appears to have played a major role in the downfall of the Nephite nation. The A.D. 350 treaty recorded in Mormon 2:28–29 was never violated by the Mayans. To this day the Maya people still live on the

Top Left: Temple of Quetzalcoatl at Teotihuacan showing the serpent motif associated with the god Quetzalcoatl. Dates to A.D. 200. The legends of Quetzalcoatl in relation to the resurrection are associated with Teotihuacan.

Top Center: View of the Avenue of the Dead in Teotihuacan showing the Pyramid of the Moon, constructed circa A.D. 400.

Top Right: The awe-inspiring Pyramid of the Sun at Teotihuacan was restored in 1910 to commemorate the 100th anniversary of Mexico's independence. The reconstruction is inferior compared to today's standards. Nevertheless, it shows the massive structure with 62 steps leading to the top, and it is one of the largest pyramids in Mesoamerica.

Above: The Pyramid of the Sun dates to the first century B.C. during the same time period that many Nephites migrated from the land of Zarahemla to the land northward (Alma 63:5). By A.D. 600, Teotihuacan boasted a population of an estimated 200,000 people. Its downfall came about as a result of secret combinations around A.D. 750. Teotihuacan also played a major role in the downfall of the Nephite nation. Evidence now exists which indicates that Teotihuacan played a major role in the downfall of the Nephite nation in the 4th century A.D.

Opposite: Obsidian figurine from Teotihuacan.

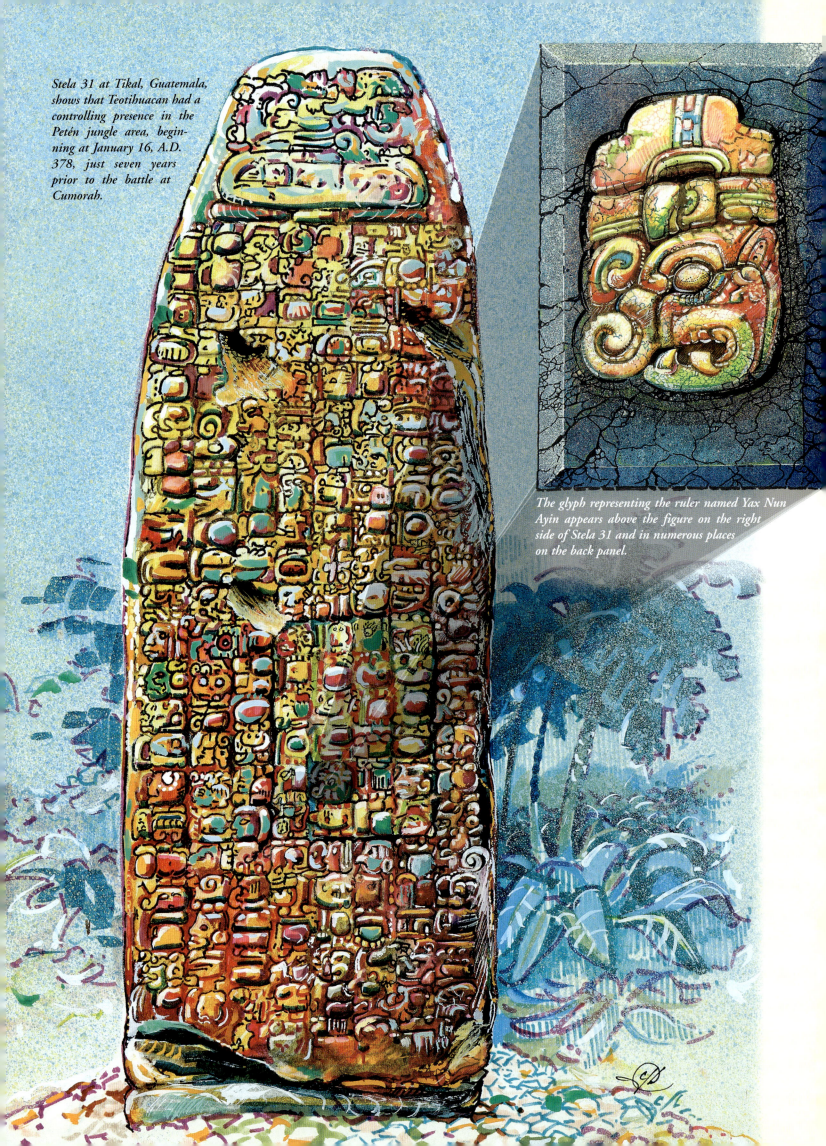

Stela 31 at Tikal, Guatemala, shows that Teotihuacan had a controlling presence in the Petén jungle area, beginning at January 16, A.D. 378, just seven years prior to the battle at Cumorah.

The glyph representing the ruler named Yax Nun Ayin appears above the figure on the right side of Stela 31 and in numerous places on the back panel.

TEOTIHUACAN 93

Left: "And I, Mormon, wrote an epistle unto the king of the Lamanites, and desired of him that he would grant unto us that we might gather together our people unto the land of Cumorah, by a hill which was called Cumorah, and there we could give them battle" (Mormon 6:2). The above king named Yax Nun Ayin, or First Crocodile, may have been the Lamanite king to whom Mormon wrote his epistle.

Below: This image (located on the right panel of Stela 31) depicts the ruler from Teotihuacan as a controlling figure in the entire Mesoamerican region at the end of the fourth century A.D. There may be an association with him and the secret combination government set up by King Jacob in the first century A.D. (3 Nephi 7:12–13).

southward side of the isthmus. It now appears that Teotihuacan, or Mexico (called the Gadianton Robbers) was the second signer of the treaty. They did violate the treaty. The Nephites were the third signer of the A.D. 350 treaty. At first they only lost a portion of their land, the land of Zarahemla and the land Bountiful. Within a few years, however, they lost their entire nation at Cumorah. They were then exiled from the land.

The king at Teotihuacan during these dark days of Nephite history was a man who is sometimes referred to as Spear Thrower Owl. He ruled Teotihuacan for sixty years. Although we don't know his real name, there is some indication that the first two letters of his name are JA. The following three letters are obliterated and are followed by a name appendage.[4] It is significant to note, however, that the name KOB is common in Mayan literature. This is purely conjecture at this time, but the JA along with KOB, the possible three missing letters, may still show the secret combination society name started by Jacob, and would still be in effect 300 years after Jacob established it.

As a true secret combination leader, and in violation of the A.D. 350 treaty, Spear Thrower Owl sent his young son to Tikal with a strong military leader called Smoking Frog, a name given because of his facial drawing on Stela 31 at Tikal. On January 18, A.D. 378, seven years before the Cumorah battle, Smoking Frog killed the Maya/Lamanite ruler named Great Jaguar Paw and placed the young son of Spear Thrower Owl on the throne at Tikal in the Land Southward. He ruled from A.D. 378–421. His Maya name is Yax Nun Ayin. It is to this king that Mormon probably wrote his epistle, proposing a battle at Cumorah (Morm. 6:2).[5] As Mormon wrote earlier:

> And behold, in the end of this book ye shall see that this Gadianton did prove the overthrow, yea, almost the entire destruction of the people of Nephi. Behold, I do not mean at the end of the book of Helaman, but I mean at the end of the book of Nephi, from which I have taken all the account which I have written (Hel. 2:13–14).

For all intents and purposes, Teotihuacan was run by secret combinations from A.D. 350–600, Teotihuacan Period III. And it was those secret combinations, according to Ignacio Bernal that brought about the downfall of Teotihuacan itself.[6]

For years I have felt we would probably understand more about secret combinations and the Gadianton robbers when as a society we were exposed to them. This is a factor common to both the Jaredite and Nephite downfall, and we would be wise to be aware of their deadly presence in our own day.

Chapter Nine
Dark and Loathsome

*After they had dwindled in unbelief they became
a dark, and loathsome, and a filthy people. (1 Nephi 12:23)*

The Mayan Classic Period and the Nephite Apostasy

    In 4 Nephi we read, "In this two hundred and first year there began to be among them those who were lifted up in pride, such as the wearing of costly apparel" (4 Nephi 1:24). It is no coincidence that the Mayan Classic period and the great Nephite apostasy began simultaneously. The Mayan Classic period embraced 700 years, from A.D. 200–900, whereas the Nephite apostasy began at A.D. 200 and culminated with the Nephite dispersion at A.D. 400. The last 200 years of the Nephites in Mesoamerica is recorded in 4 Nephi and Mormon.

    The Nephites reported a millennial lifestyle that lasted almost 166 years following the coming of Christ. Perhaps the first half of 4 Nephi is a prophetic parallel of the millennium we look forward to and the Second Coming of the Prince of Peace. It may also be prophesying of the end of the Millennium when Satan will be loosed for a season, just as he was he loosed among the Nephites beginning at A.D. 201, gaining great "hold upon their hearts" (4 Ne. 1:28).

Above: Sites such as Uxmal, Copan, and Palenque began to surface between A.D. 200 and A.D. 400. See locations on the map.

Opposite: "And it came to pass that I beheld, after they had dwindled in unbelief they became a dark, and loathsome, and a filthy people, full of idleness and all manner of abominations" (1 Nephi 12:23). The Maya priests controlled the spiritual, social and economic affairs of the people during the Classic Maya time period. Religion was reduced to idolatry, and the common people suffered immensely under this political structure. The above drawing by Frederick Catherwood of the Well of Bolonchin in the Yucatan peninsula shows the subservient demeanor of the people, which lasted for over 1000 years, right up to the coming of the Spaniards in the 16th century.

THE NEPHITE PRIESTS

Between A.D. 201 and 320 the Nephites no longer had things in common and a religious hierarchy developed. The people were led by many priests and "false prophets who were lifted up in pride and began to wear costly apparel and all manner of fine things" (4 Ne. 1:24, 34). Led by the wicked priests, the people built up churches and adorned them with all manner of precious things. Secret combinations again surfaced in the land, and the Gadianton robbers "did lay up in store" gold and silver and did "traffic in all manner of traffic" (4 Ne. 1:41, 46).

It is my opinion that those wicked priests, for the most part, were the same people who in the first century B.C. wanted to establish a kingship in the land. They appear to be those who were of Jewish descent, including descendants of Zoram and Mulek. For over 400 years we witness the partial fulfillment of the prophecy of Joseph of Egypt, wherein his brothers would bow down to him. Beginning with Mosiah, the Mulekites and the Zoramites (descendants of Judah) went to the Nephites (descendants of Joseph) for both temporal and spiritual leadership.

This is consistent with the Mesoamerican picture. The Mayan royalty of 200 B.C. had their beginnings in the middle of the first century B.C., just like the A.D. 200 wicked Nephite (Mulekite) priests had their beginnings with the 67 B.C. king-men (Alma 51:8).

Eventually this all changed, and by A.D. 320, the end of 4 Nephi, the apostasy was in full effect. This is the same time that the Great Apostasy took place in the old world. In other words, Satan was working on opposite sides of the world with the exact same tactics. During A.D. 400, Moroni informs us that the Lamanites put to death all of those who would not deny the Christ. This suggests that perhaps Moroni was not the only one who had to flee the area. Like the Jewish dispersion at A.D. 70, there appears to have been a Nephite dispersion at A.D. 400.

THE MAYANS

Evidence shows that what is recorded in the Nephite record is precisely what happened throughout Mesoamerica during the same time period. The archaeological zone of Uxmal, for example, shows that at A.D. 200 there was a great division among the people, and the Maya priests were the people spoken of in 4 Nephi who began to wear costly apparel. The archaeological report reads:

> During this period [early Classic A.D. 200–350], the dominant group was a hereditary elite which emerged in the last century before Christ. Its authority extended throughout all aspects of social life, but in particular they were representatives or mediators between the community and the divine or supernatural forces, utilizing magical/religious means. This group controlled the knowledge of the times, much of which, in order to maintain a relationship with the direct production of the people, determined social behavior.[1]

DARK AND LOATHSOME 97

"In this two hundred and first year there began to be among them those who were lifted up in pride, such as the wearing of costly apparel, and all manner of fine pearls, and of the fine things of the world. . . . And they began to be divided into classes; and they began to build up churches unto themselves to get gain, and began to deny the true church of Christ" (4 Nephi 1:24, 26). A hierarchy consisting of Maya and Teotihuacan royalty began to dominate the Mesoamerica scene as stated in 4 Nephi and as depicted in this illustration representing the different classes among the Maya.

Above: Elaborately adorned building in Uxmal (Catherwood). "And they did still continue to build up churches unto themselves, and adorn them with all manner of precious things. And thus did two hundred and fifty years pass away" (4 Nephi 1:41). This date represents the beginning of the Maya Classic period and is directly related to the great Nephite apostasy.

At the time of the Spanish conquest in what today is Mexico City, human sacrifices were being performed by the Aztec priests, a practice that began as early as the fourth century A.D. in the Book of Mormon (Mormon 4:14–15, 21). Bernal Diaz, a soldier in the army of Cortez, reported that the priests would cut out the heart of the sacrificial victims with a sharp obsidian knife like the one shown here.

The report continues:

> This period runs from A.D. 200–1000 and has been called the period of the Theocratic States Monopoly by virtue of the fact that the high priests controlled and monopolized the main activities or the social and economic life of the population, encompassing even the simple ritualism, symbolism and beliefs.[2]

At the beginning of the Mayan Classic period A.D. 200, a massive building program began and continued for several centuries. Over the years, many of the buildings were nothing more than elaborately adorned tombs prepared for the priests/kings by the lower-class workforce. Places at Palenque, Tikal, Monte Albán, Teotihuacan, Copan, Yaxchilan, Calakmul, and many other sites that were built after A.D. 200 began to flourish. It was about A.D. 322 when Mormon said his father took him to the Land Southward and the whole face of the land was "covered with buildings, and the people were as numerous almost, as it were the sand of the sea (Morm. 1:7).

Wars were rampant during the great Nephite apostasy and early Classic Mayan era. At A.D. 331, Mormon reported that "it was one complete revolution through all the face of the land" (Morm. 2:8). And at A.D. 400, Moroni wrote that the Lamanite "wars are exceedingly fierce among themselves" (Moro. 1:2). In recent years Maya archaeologists have concluded that the Maya were not a peaceful people as had earlier been reported, but they were in continual warfare with one another. There can be little doubt that the Mayans and the Lamanites were the same people during the Mayan Classic period. However, the rulers of their dynasties (dynasties that lasted until the ninth century A.D.) may have been of Jewish descent. This is not meant to imply that the Lamanites, descendants of Laman and Lemuel, were of the tribe of Judah, because they were not. They were of the tribe of Joseph. Of course the descendants of the Jaredites were not of the tribe of Judah either. It does imply that after A.D. 400 Lamanites, deserted Nephites, Mulekites, descendants of the Jaredites, and any other people who lived in the area southward of the Isthmus of Tehuantepec fell under the Lamanite/Mayan umbrella.

I propose, however, that the descendants of the king-men were none other than the descendants of Judah that created the great Mayan dynasty from A.D. 200–900, the Maya Classic period. I base this assumption on the activities of two kings in the Book of Mormon, Amalickiah and Jacob, both of whom were apparently descendants of the tribe of Judah, and from archaeological evidence relating to the respective time periods. The treacherous Amalickiah and his successors were descendants of Zoram, who as near as can be determined was a descendant of Judah (Alma 54:23). You will recall it was Amalickiah who cunningly became king over the entire Lamanite nation in the middle of the first century B.C. And likewise, the wicked King Jacob fled into the Land Northward in the first century A.D. and there established a "secret combination" government. As near as can be determined, Jacob was a descendant of Mulek, and hence Judah.

Archaeological evidence supports the intrusion of a dynasty from Teotihuacan into Mayan territory in the latter part of the fourth century A.D., which resulted in the demise of the Nephites as recorded in the Book of Mormon, as well as the termination of the Nephite history.[3]

Dark and Loathsome

I propose that it was the middle Classic A.D. 400 Mayans that the great prophet Nephi saw in vision 600 years before the birth of Christ, when he wrote:

> And I, Nephi, also saw many of the fourth generation who passed away in righteousness. . . . And it came to pass that I looked and beheld the people of my seed gathered together in multitudes against the seed of my brethren; and they were gathered together in battle (1 Ne. 12:12, 15).
>
> And because of the pride of my seed, and the temptations of the devil, I beheld that the seed of my brethren did overpower the people of my seed . . . and I saw wars and rumors of wars among them. (1 Ne. 12:19, 21; see Mormon 6 and Moro. 1:1 for the fulfillment of that prophecy.)

Furthermore, I propose that it was the late Classic and post-Classic (A.D. 700–1500) Mayans to whom Nephi was referring when he wrote:

> I saw many generations pass away . . . And it came to pass that I beheld, after they had dwindled in unbelief they became a *dark*, and *loathsome*, and *filthy* people, full of idleness and all manner of abominations (1 Ne. 12:23, emphasis added).

It was during the fourth century A.D. when Mormon reported that the Lamanites took women and children as prisoners and offered them as sacrifices to their idol gods (Mormon 4:14–15, 21). And in an epistle to his son Moroni, he wrote that the Lamanites "feed the women upon the flesh of their husbands, and the children upon the flesh of their fathers" (Moro. 9:8). The Nephite soldiers were equal to, if not worse than the Lamanites, as they deprived the Lamanite women prisoners of that which was most dear and precious, which was their virtue, and then murdered and tortured their bodies and "devour[ed] their flesh like unto wild beasts, because of the hardness of their hearts; and they do it for a token of bravery." Mormon then said that "[they] are without civilization" (Moro. 9:10–11).

It is impossible to imagine the uncivilized atrocities that took place in the world of Mesoamerica from the close of the Book of Mormon to the coming of the Spaniards in the sixteenth century A.D. This does not mean that people living in other parts of America during the above-mentioned time were not doing some of the same things that the Mayans, Toltecs, and Aztecs were doing. It just means that a high concentration of people in the Americas during this time period lived in Mesoamerica. Even today, for every Native American who lives north of the Rio Grande, there are an estimated 100 people living in the area of Mesoamerica. The climate and food supply probably account for that population unbalance during the time period of the Book of Mormon.

Bernal Diaz, a soldier in the army of Cortez, reported the commonality of human sacrifice among the Aztecs in the sixteenth century. He wrote that on sacrificial days the priests had their long black hair matted in blood, would cut out the heart of the victim with one swoop of their sharp obsidian knife. And, with the heart still beating, they would hold it up to the sun god.[4]

In the name of religion, Mayan activities during the Classic and post-Classic periods were diabolical in another dimension. The ceremony of bloodletting was indeed bizarre, as among the women it consisted of drawing a small rope through their tongue to extract blood to offer to their gods. The male would do the same, only through the male organ. This apparently was meant to accomplish two things. (1) It proved their submission and dedication to their gods, and (2) it provided a means whereby the priests themselves could take the place of God. In other words, they apparently conceived the idea that they could resurrect themselves by giving their own blood, thus taking the place of the Savior.[5]

The words "black, dark, filthy, and loathsome" are synonymous in the Book of Mormon. They describe the spiritual condition of people who forsake the commandments of God. The words "skins" and "garments," when used in a spiritual context, refer to one's inner soul, such as, "the Lord did cause a skin of blackness to come upon them" (2 Ne. 5:21),[6] or "unless ye shall repent of your sins, their skins will be whiter than yours" (Jacob 3:8), or "their skin became white like unto the Nephites" (3 Ne. 2:15). And the Lord promised through Nephi, that in the latter days the "scales of darkness" would begin to fall from their eyes and they would become a "pure and delightsome people" (2 Ne. 30:6).[7]

Chapter Ten
Pure and Delightsome

Their scales of darkness shall begin to fall from their eyes; and many generations shall not pass away among them, save they shall be a pure and a delightsome people. (2 Nephi 30:6)

The Spanish Conquest and the Arrival of the Pilgrims

Two events took place that determined the modern history of two countries. The events are the coming of the Spaniards and the arrival of the Pilgrims. The two countries are the United States of America and Los Estados Unidos de Mexico. The two countries are so close, yet so different. The difference prompted one author to write a book called *Distant Neighbors*.[1] The language of one country is Spanish and the other is English. Mexico has remained fairly isolated, maintaining an estimated 85 percent native bloodline in their veins, while the United States has become a melting pot of nations with less than 15 percent of native blood within its population. The population of Mexico, combined with the other Central American countries that constituted ancient Mesoamerica, is 150 million. The United States boasts more than twice that number. It is estimated that over 20 million people living in the United States have ties with Mexico and Central America. The traditional religion of Mexico, over the last 500 years, is Catholicism, whereas the United States has supported a Protestant tradition.

Above: The map highlights the areas on the Mesoamerica map where, in recent years, Latter-day Saint temples have been built. The purpose of this chapter is to provide a feeling of the fulfillment of prophecy among the physical and spiritual descendants of Lehi that has taken place from 1521 to the present day.

Opposite: Guatemala City Temple. Nephi built a temple in the City of Nephi shortly after their arrival in the promised land around 560 B.C. Now, 2500 years later, a temple has been built in the latter days in what appears to have been the same land where Nephi built a temple unto the Lord (2 Ne. 5:16).

102 SACRED SITES

The origin of the two nations mentioned above is spelled out in prophecy by Nephi as recorded in 1 Nephi 13:1–19. This section is written in Hebrew poetic style. The first half prophesies of the Spanish conquest, and the second half portrays the coming of the Pilgrims from England.

SPAIN

Regarding the Spanish conquest, Nephi saw the following:

(1) He saw many nations and kingdoms of the Gentiles, though this appears to refer specifically to the European nations. One of these nations was Spain.

Far Above: Guatemalan Church member from Patzicia, Chimal Tenango, carrying her young child on her back. A stake of the Church has now been organized in this community.

Above: Villahermosa Temple. Located in the State of Tabasco, Mexico, Villahermosa is the dividing line of the Maya and the Olmecs. This temple took two years to build and was dedicated on May 21, 2000.

Right: Mexico City Temple. Dedicated on December 2, 1983, after seven years of construction. The Mexico City Temple was the first to be built in the area that has been considered in this work as the lands of the Book of Mormon.

(2) He saw the formation of a great church among the nations of the Gentiles. Historically, the mother church of Europe in the sixteenth century was the Christian church.

(3) He saw that the gold, silver, silks, and scarlets were the things which this church most desired, calling them "great and abominable." Within a spiritual framework, however, there are only two churches; one is of Christ and the other is of the devil (1 Ne. 14:10).

(4) He saw many waters that divided the Gentiles from the seed of his brethren. It is the Atlantic Ocean that divides Spain from Mexico.

(5) He saw that the Spirit of God wrought upon a man among the Gentiles who was separated from the seed of the brethren of Nephi. This man is usually referred to as Columbus. He is reported as saying the following.

> The Lord was well disposed to my desire, and he bestowed upon me courage and understanding, knowledge of seafaring. He gave me in abundance, of astrology as much as was needed, and of geometry and astronomy likewise. Further, he gave me cunning in drawing maps. I have seen and truly I have studied books, histories, chronicles, and philosophies, and other arts, for which the Lord unlocked my mind, sent me upon the sea, and gave me fire for the deed. Those who heard of my enterprise called it foolish, mocked me, and laughed. But who can doubt that the Holy Ghost inspired me.[2]

In the year 1519, twenty-seven years after Columbus discovered America, another Spaniard by the name of Hernan Cortez, with a small fleet of ships, approximately 400 soldiers, some horses, cannons, and a supply of gunpowder, anchored off the coast of Veracruz, Mexico. They moved inland with a translator named Doña Marina and thousands of native foot soldiers whose hatred for the Aztecs was unparalleled. Upon their arrival in the ancient city of Tenochtitlan, which today is downtown Mexico City, he was permitted to enter because Mocteczuma is reported as having mistaken them for Quetzalcoatl or the sons of Quetzalcoatl. The conquest was long and bloody and in September of 1521, the seed of the brethren of Nephi were "scattered before the Gentiles and were smitten" (1 Ne. 13:14).

The Spaniards brought with them a book which had proceeded "out of the mouth of the Jew," the Bible (1 Ne. 13:33). However, their conversion tactics consisted of force. Elaborate churches arose in every village, just as elaborate buildings had arisen during the Mayan Classic period. The seed of Lehi was now in bondage to another people, and that bondage lasted until 1810 when Mexico gained their independence from Spain. However, a century would pass before another book would be carried to the seed of Lehi by another group of Gentiles. That book is the Book of Mormon.

ENGLAND

Nephi also saw in vision the establishment of a free society a century after the Spanish conquest of Mexico. However, the motive of this second group was much different. Whereas the Spanish moved into Mexico and Central America and placed the seed of Lehi in bondage, those who came from England did so to escape bondage and gain religious freedom. The following represents what Nephi saw in vision recorded in 1 Nephi 13.

(1) He saw the Spirit of God that it wrought upon other Gentiles and they went forth out of captivity upon the many waters (1 Ne. 13:13). This group came from England and neighboring countries. They crossed the Atlantic Ocean and arrived at Plymouth Rock in 1620.

(2) He saw that the Spirit of the Lord was with the Gentiles who had come out of captivity and they did prosper and obtain the land for their inheritance (1 Ne. 13:14). From the inception of the history of the United States this has been the case.

(3) He saw that the Gentiles who came forth out of captivity did humble themselves before the Lord and the power of the Lord was with them (1 Ne. 13:12). The Constitution of the United States of America is considered to be an inspired document. The Restoration of the gospel through the Prophet Joseph Smith came about as a result of humble prayer.

(4) He saw their mother Gentiles gathered together upon the many waters to do battle. The Gentiles that had gone out of captivity were delivered by the power of God out of the hands of all other nations (1 Ne. 13:17–19). The Revolutionary War was in 1776 when the United States of America gained their independence.

PURE AND DELIGHTSOME

In speaking to his people, the Prophet Nephi said:

> And now, I would prophesy somewhat more concerning the Jews and the Gentiles. For after the book of which I have spoken [the Book of Mormon] shall come forth, and be written unto the Gentiles [early Latter-day Saints], and sealed up again unto the Lord, there shall be many which shall believe the words which are written; and they [LDS missionaries] shall carry them forth unto the remnant of our seed.
>
> And the gospel of Jesus Christ shall be declared among them (descendants of Lehi); wherefore, they shall be restored unto the knowledge of their fathers, and also to the knowledge of Jesus Christ, which was had among their fathers (2 Ne. 30:5).

Samuel the Lamanite, speaking of the restoration of the truth to his brethren, the Lamanites, in the latter-days wrote: "Yea, even if they should dwindle in unbelief the Lord will prolong their days, until the time shall come which hath been spoken of by our fathers" (Hel. 15:11).

I believe that prophecy is history in reverse. Mormon wrote; "I also know that as many things as have been prophesied concerning us down to this day have been fulfilled, and as many as go beyond this day must surely come to pass" (W of M 1:4). It therefore stands to reason that the fulfillment of these prophecies in our day may indirectly help us in understanding where the history outlined in the Book of Mormon took place. In summary, there are six events in the history of the United States and Mexico that stand out as landmark cases in bringing to pass that which was prophesied by the prophets of old, some of have which have already been discussed.

(1) The discovery of America by Columbus, that "man among the Gentiles" who was inspired by the Spirit of God to cross the many waters to the promised land (1 Ne. 13:12).

(2) The conquest of Mexico by Cortez who, in the name of Christianity, conquered and scattered those who were upon the promised land (1 Ne. 13:14). Mexico remained in spiritual bondage for 336 years, from 1521 to 1857. Nevertheless, Catholicism introduced the Bible to the seed of Lehi and to people throughout all the Americas that were conquered by Spain.

(3) The arrival of the pilgrims who "went out of captivity" from England to the new world. Nephi wrote that he "beheld the Spirit of the Lord, upon the Gentiles, and they did prosper" and they were "white and exceedingly fair and beautiful" like unto his people before they were slain. The power of God was with the Gentiles and they were delivered by the power of God out of the hands of all other nations. Nephi saw in vision a book, meaning the Bible, that was carried forth among them (1 Ne. 13:15–20).

(4) The restoration of the gospel through Joseph Smith, that "choice seer" who would do a work of great worth unto bringing the remnant of Jacob to a knowledge of the covenants that God has made with them (2 Ne. 3:7). Furthermore, the establishment of the Church under the direction of Brigham Young in the "tops of the mountains" as prophesied by the Prophet Isaiah (Isa. 2:2; 2 Ne.12:2).

(5) Mexico's war of independence with Spain, wherein a Catholic priest by the name of Miguel Hidalgo sounded the church bells which initiated a march to Mexico City that subsequently brought a close to Spain's rule in Mexico. Mexico gained her independence on September 16, 1810, just a few years prior to the First Vision of Joseph Smith.

(6) Reform laws were drafted in 1857 by Benito Juarez, which resulted in the separation of church and state and which ultimately made it possible for the restored gospel to be preached throughout Mexico.

BENITO JUAREZ

Benito Juarez was born on March 21, 1806, three months after the birth of the Prophet Joseph Smith. He was born in the mountains of Oaxaca and was a Zapotec Indian from that state. He was a serious student and studied the clergy as well as law. He became governor of Oaxaca in 1847, the same year the Saints crossed the

This large mural of Benito Juarez is located at the crossroads leading to the mountain village of Oaxaca where he was born. From left to right, it shows him as a young sheepherder, a student, governor of Oaxaca, author of the "Reform Laws," president of Mexico. It also shows the fall from power of the Catholic Church (lower right), and the defeat of the French invasion under the emperor Maximillian (also lower right).

plains and Brigham Young became governor of the territory of Deseret. Juarez was elected president of Mexico in 1861, the only native to ever hold that position, and in 1862, he victoriously led his people against the French invaders at the battle of "cinco de mayo," but then suffered defeat in the war, which allowed for the intrusion of Maximilian. Five years later, Juarez defeated Maximilian, regained the presidency, and put into action the Reform Laws mentioned above.

The Lord's hand is seen on both sides of the border. (1) American members of the Church established themselves in northern Mexico, which has become known as the Mormon colonies. These members, holding dual citizenship, have provided the leadership necessary to establish a firm foundation for the growth of the Church in Mexico. And (2), the laws enacted by Juarez have made it possible for the gospel to be preached to "that remnant of Jacob."

The growth of the Church in Mexico and other parts of Latin America has indeed been marvelous over the last half century. Thousands, and hundreds of thousands have been baptized into the Church. A high percentage of the missionary force is now native to their respective countries. Stakes dot the entire land, and in recent years, temples have been built to accommodate the faithful Saints. A Church-sponsored high school in Mexico City, consisting of 3,000 students, prepares young members for missionary service and temple marriage.

As history has borne out, we have seen great and marvelous things accomplished since the restoration of the gospel in 1830, as promised by the Lord to his ancient prophet Lehi. And we can anticipate with excitement the fulfillment of other wonderful events that have been prophesied to precede the Savior's Second Coming and the ushering in of the glorious resurrection.

END NOTES

INTRODUCTION: SACRED GEOGRAPHY
1. Joseph L. Allen, *Exploring the Lands of the Book of Mormon* (Provo, UT: S.A. Publishers, 1989), 10.
2. Ibid., 4–6.
3. John Lloyd Stephens, *Incidents of Travel in Central America, Chiapas, and Yucatan,* 2 vols. (1831; reprint, New York: Dover Publications, 1969).
4. "Article Title," *Times and Seasons,* date, 927. *Times and Seasons* was the official Church publication from 1839–46. Joseph Smith, Jr., and John Taylor were the editors of the 1842 volume, which included several citations from the writings of John Lloyd Stephens.

CHAPTER 1: LEHI'S LANDING SITE
1. Kent S. Brown, "New Light from Arabia on Lehi's Trail," in *Echoes and Evidences of the Book of Mormon,* eds. Donald W. Parry, Daniel C. Peterson, and John W. Welch (Provo, UT: Farms, 2002), 55–125.
2. Allen, "The Voyage of Lehi's Colony," in *Exploring the Lands of the Book of Mormon,* 263–70.
3. V. Garth Norman, *Izapa Sculpture,* Papers of the New World Archaeological Foundation, vol. 30 (Provo, UT: New World Archaeological Foundation, 1976), 1. See also Allen, *Exploring the Lands of the Book of Mormon,* 117.
4. Gareth W. Lowe, Thomas A. Lee, and Eduardo Martinez Espinosa, *Izapa: An Introduction to the Ruins and Monuments,* Papers of the New World Archaeological Foundation, vol. 31 (Provo, UT: New World Archaeological Foundation, 1982), page. See also Allen, *Exploring the Lands of the Book of Mormon,* 111–15.
5. Norman, *Izapa Sculpture,* 329.
6. John E. Clark and Stewart W. Brewer, "Article Title," *Journal of Book of Mormon Studies* 8, no. 1 (1999): pages. See also V. Garth Norman et al., "Tree of Life Stone Under Attack," *Book of Mormon Archaeological Digest* 2, no. 4 (1999): pages.
7. Joseph L. Allen, David C. Asay, and Chris Heimerdinger, *Lehi's Land of First Inheritance,* (Orem, UT: Book of Mormon Archaeological Foundation, 2002), documentary.
8. Allen J. Christenson, ed. and trans., *Popul Vuh; The Mythic Sections-Tales of First Beginnings from the Ancient K'iche'—Maya* (Provo, UT: Farms, 2000). The Popul Vuh is a pre-Columbian text originally written by anonymous members of the K'iche'-Maya nobility who lived in the western Maya highlands of Guatemala.
9. V. Garth Norman, "Where Was the Land of First Inheritance?" *Book of Mormon Archaeological Digest* vol, no. 1 (1991): 15–17.
10. Alberto Ruz Lhuillier. *The Maya* (City, Mexico: Salvat mexicana de Ediciones, 1983). See also Allen, *Exploring the Lands of the Book of Mormon,* 36.
11. Joseph Gorrell, "Serpents and Flocks," *Book of Mormon Archaeological Digest* vol, no. # (2001): 12–13.

CHAPTER 2: UP TO NEPHI
1. Allen, *Exploring the Lands of the Book of Mormon,* 73. See also Jace Willard, "Kaminaljuyu and the City of Nephi: Seven Reasons for Taking a Closer Look," *Explorations in the Book of Mormon* (City: State, Publisher, 1999), 125–34.
2. John Eric Sidney Thompson, *The Rise and Fall of the Maya Civilization,* 2d ed. (Norman, OK: Univ. of Oklahoma Press), 189.
3. Author/Editor, *The Pennsylvania State University Kaminaljuyu Project* (University Park, PA: Pennsylvania State Univ. Press, 1973), 8.
4. Alfred V. Kidder, Jesse J. Jennings, and Edwin M. Shook, introduction to *Excavations at Kaminaljuyu, Guatemala* (University Park, PA: Pennsylvania State Univ. Press, 1946).
5. Author/Editor, *The Pennsylvania State University Kaminaljuyu Project,* 82.
6. Ibid., 241.
7. Ibid., 82.
8. For more information on the Land of Nephi, see Allen, "The Land of Nephi," in *Exploring the Lands of the Book of Mormon,* 359–70.
9. Bruce W. Warren and Thomas S. Ferguson, *Messiah in Ancient America* (Provo, UT: Book of Mormon Research Foundation, 1987), 44.

CHAPTER 3: DOWN TO ZARAHEMLA
1. Munro S. Edmunson, *The Book of the Year: Middle American Calendrical Systems* (Salt Lake City, UT: Univ. of Utah Press, 1988), 27.
2. Allen, *Exploring the Lands of the Book of Mormon,* 173.

CHAPTER 4: EAST WILDERNESS
1. Skousen, "A Systematic Text of the Book of Mormon," 59. In the current text of the Book of Mormon, Alma 53:6 states that the city of Mulek became one of the strongest holds of the Lamanites in the Land of Nephi. However, the city of Mulek is not in the Land of Nephi. The city of Mulek was Nephite territory. A close analysis of the original manuscripts of the Book of Mormon reveals that Oliver Cowdery interchanged the term "the people of Nephi" with "the people of the Nephites." This suggests that the passage in Alma 53:6 should more accurately read that the Lamanites had gained a stronghold in the land of the Nephites, not in the Land of Nephi.
2. Dennis E. Pulleston and Donald W. Callender, "Defensive Earth Works at Tikal," *The Archaeological Journal* 9, no. # (1967): 40–48. Also reported in Allen, *Exploring the Lands of the Book of Mormon,* 300–302. See also Ted D. Stoddard, "Moroni's Fortifications," *Explorations in the Book of Mormon,* 101–9.

Chapter 5: The Land of Bountiful

1. Allen, *Exploring the Lands of the Book of Mormon,* 139.
2. Ibid., 140, v. 16.
3. Bruce W. Warren, "One Ben, Six Mak, Thursday, April 6, 1 B.C." *Book of Mormon Archaeological Digest* 2, no. 2 (1999): 1, 7.
4. Allen, *Exploring the Lands of the Book of Mormon,* 145, v. 39.
5. Joseph L. Allen, "A Comparative Study of Quetzacoatl, the Feathered-Serpent God of Meso-America, with Jesus Christ, the God of the Nephites," (Ph.D. diss., Brigham Young University, year).
6. Constance Irwin, "Mexico's Fair God Quetzalcoatl," in *Fair Gods and Stone Faces* (New York: St. Martin's Press, 1963), 33.
7. Allen, *Exploring the Lands of the Book of Mormon,* 147, v. 45.
8. Allen, "A Comparative Study of Quetzalcoatl," 120–34.
9. Author, *Title* (Publication info).

Chapter 6: The Land of Desolation

1. Fray Bernardino de Sahugan, *Historia General de las Cosas de Nueva Espana: Florentine Codex,* 12 vols. ed. and trans. Arthur O. Anderson and Charles E. Dibble (Santa Fe, NM: School of American Research, 1950). See also Juan de Torquemada, "Monarchia Indiana," in *Myths and Languages,* ed. Hubert Howe Bancroft, The Native Races, vol. 3 (San Francisco: Bancroft, 1883), 254–55; and Allen, "The Voyage of the Mulekites," in *Exploring the Lands of the Book of Mormon,* 271–78. Sahagun and Torquemada were two of a number of Spanish chroniclers (Catholic priests) who wrote about the traditions, legends, and history of ancient Mexico.
2. Cyrus H. Gordon, *Before Columbus* (New York: Crown Books, 1971).
3. Allen, *Exploring the Lands of the Book of Mormon,* 295.
4. Ibid., 327–35.
5. David Stuart, "The Arrival of Strangers: Teotihuacan and Tollan in Classic Maya History," in *Mesoamerica's Classic Heritage: From Teotihuacan to the Aztecs,* ed. David Carrasco, Lindsay Jones, and Scott Sessions, (Princeton: Princeton Univ. Press, 2000), 465–514.
6. David A. Palmer, *In Search of Cumorah: New Evidences for the Book of Mormon from Ancient Mexico* (Bountiful, UT: Horizon, 1981), 91. John L. Sorenson, *An Ancient American Setting for the Book of Mormon* (Salt Lake City, UT: Deseret Book, 1985), 121–22.
7. Allen, *Exploring the Lands of the Book of Mormon,* 337–39.
8. Allen, "Voyage of the Jaredites," in *Exploring the Lands of the Book of Mormon,* 257–62.
9. Michael D. Coe, *The Maya* (New York: Thames and Hudson, 1981), 6.
10. Allen, *Exploring the Lands of the Book of Mormon,* 57.
11. Michael D. Coe, *Mexico* (New York: Praeger Publishers, 1962), 90.
12. Allen, *Exploring the Lands of the Book of Mormon,* page. See also Milton R. Hunter and Thomas Stuart Ferguson, "chapter 15 title," in *Ancient America and the Book of Mormon* (Oakland, CA: Kolob Book, 1950), inclusive pages.
13. Allen, *Exploring the Lands of the Book of Mormon,* 139, v. 7.
14. Ibid., 139, v. 8.
15. Ibid., 141, v. 21
16. Ibid.
17. Ibid., 141, v. 22; 122, v. 24.
18. Ibid., 142, v. 25–26.
19. Ibid., 140, v. 16; 142, v. 25, 28.
20. Ibid., 146, v. 41.

Chapter 7: Monte Albán

1. Ignacio Bernal, *Valle de Oaxaca* (city, Mexico: Hachette Latino-America, 1992).
2. Allen, "The Zapotec/Mulekite Culture," *Exploring the Lands of the Book of Mormon,* 85–95.
3. Bernal, *Valle de Oaxaca.*
4. Ibid., 22, as quoted in Joseph L. Allen, *Exploring the Lands of the Book of Mormon,* 92.
5. Allen, "A Comparative Study of Quetzalcoatl," 8–12.
6. Bernal, *Valle de Oaxaca,* 24–26.
7. Ibid., 28.
8. Ibid., 27.
9. Ibid., 23.
10. Allen, *Exploring the Lands of the Book of Mormon,* 92.

Chapter 8: Teotihuacan

1. Sahugan, *Historia General de las Cosas de Nueva Espana.*
2. Joseph L. Allen, "Hagoth: 56–45 B.C.," *Book of Mormon Archaeological Digest* vol, no. # (year): 12.
3. Shele and Friedel, *A Forest of Kings,* 142–45. This portrays the date of a Tikal ruler who ascended the throne on September 17, 300, the last year date recorded in 4 Nephi.
4. Nikoli Gruebei, *title* (city, state: publisher, year).
5. Stuart, "The Arrival of Strangers," 465–514. See also author, "Mormon's Epistle to Yax Ayin," *Book of Mormon Archaeological Digest* 3, no. 2 (2001): 1–5.
6. Allen, "Teotihuacan Culture," *Exploring the Lands of the Book of Mormon,* 97–107.

Chapter 9: Dark and Loathsome

1. Ignacio Bernal, *book title* (city, state: publisher, 1986), 32, as quoted in Joseph L. Allen, *Exploring the Lands of the Book of Mormon,* 392.
2. Bernal, *book title,* 32, as quoted in Allen, *Exploring the Lands of the Book of Mormon,* 393.
3. Stuart, "The Arrival of Strangers," 465–514.
4. Bernal de Castillo Diaz, *The Conquest of New Spain,* trans. J. M. Cohen, (city, state: Penguin, 1963).
5. David Freidel, Linda Shele, and Joy Parker, *Maya Cosmos* (New York: Morrow, 1995), 204–7. See also Blain Yorgason, Bruce W. Warren, and Harold Brown, *The Messiah Redeemer in Ancient America* (city, state: publisher, year).
6. Alan Miner, "A Skin of Blackness," *Book of Mormon Archaeological Digest* 4, no. 1 (2002): 5–7.
7. Clate Mask, "White and Delightsome," *Book of Mormon Archaeological Digest* 4, no. 1 (2002): 1, 3–4.

Chapter 10: Pure and Delightsome

1. Alan Riding, *Distant Neighbors: A Portrait of the Mexicans* (New York: Vintage Books, 1984).
2. Jacob Wasserman, *Columbus, Don Quixote of the Seas* (city, state: publisher, year), 19.

Illustration & Photo Credits

Front Endsheet map drawing without text © Cliff Dunstan.
iv Purple flower, © Phil Skousen.
1   Glyph borders, © Cliff Dunstan.
2   Relief map, by Mark Peterson.
3   "It Came to Pass" glyph, © Cliff Dunstan; photo © Merrill C. Oaks.
3   Ruins of Palenque, © Phil Skousen.
4   Leather panel, photography by Leon Woodward
6   Olmec artifacts (all), © Phil Skousen.
7   Mayan dignitaries from Chiapas, © Merrill C. Oaks.
8   Feathered serpent from Temple of Quetzalcoatl, © Phil Skousen.
9   *Teocallis at Chichen Itza,* by Frederick Catherwood, *Views of Ancient Monuments in Central America, Chiapas and Yucatan,* 1844, London: Archivio White Star.
9   Olmec relief sculpture, © Phil Skousen.
10 Cranes in trees, © Phil Skousen.
10 Yellow flower, © Phil Skousen.
10 Tacana volcano, © Phil Skousen.
10 Ruins of Abaj Takalik, © Phil Skousen.
11 Hill Cumorah/Joseph Smith, © Cliff Dunstan.
12 Mayan sculpture, photography by Leon Woodward.
12 Olmec head, © Phil Skousen.
13 Lake Catemaco, © Phil Skousen.
13 *Temple at Tulum,* by Frederick Catherwood, *Views of Ancient Monuments in Central America, Chiapas and Yucatan,* 1844, London: Archivio White Star.
16 *Izapa, Stela 5,* © Cliff Dunstan.
18 Frankincense resin, photography by Leon Woodward.
18 Old city of Jerusalem, © Paul Cheesman.
19 Sands of Sinai Desert, © D. Kelly Ogden.
19 Red Sea, © Floyd Holdman.
19 Camel Caravan, © Floyd Holdman.
19 Map showing Lehi's trail © Cliff Dunstan.
20 Soconusco valley, © Phil Skousen.
21 Goat water bag, photography by Leon Woodward.
22 Izapa, © Merrill C. Oaks.
22 Stela 5, © Phil Skousen.
23 *Izapa, Stela 5,* © Cliff Dunstan.
24 Olmec mask, photography by Leon Woodward.
24 Children with cocoa pod, © Phil Skousen.
25 Jade serpent, photography by Leon Woodward.
26 Cornfields in Guatemala, © Phil Skousen.
29 *Altar 10 at Kaminaljuyu,* © Cliff Dunstan.
30 Grassy mound at Kaminaljuyu, © Phil Skousen.
30 Model of Kaminaljuyu photo by Robert Hawkes.
32 Ruins at Kaminaljuyu, © Merrill C. Oaks.
33 Corn field, © Phil Skousen.
33 Ix'imche ruins, © Phil Skousen.
33 Highlands of Guatemala, © Merrill C. Oaks.
34 Lake Atitlán, © Phil Skousen??
35 Native Guatemalans (all three), © Merrill C. Oaks.
36 Girls with goats in Guatemalan highlands, © Phil Skousen.
38 Woman from Almolonga, © Phil Skousen.
38 Village of Almolonga, © Phil Skousen.
39 Wood carving, photography by Leon Woodward.
39 Native Guatemalan carrying bundle, © Merrill C. Oaks.
40 Guatemalan women washing clothes in a stream, © Paul Cheesman.
41 Corn field and volcano, © Phil Skousen.
42 Waterfalls near Lake Atitlán, © Phil Skousen.
44 Ruins of Zaculeu, © Merrill C. Oaks.
45 Jade Olmec figurine, photography by Leon Woodward.
46 Lagoons in Tabasco and Campeche, © Merrill C. Oaks.
46 Mountain range dividing Guatemala and Chiapas, by Clark Butterfield.
47 Relief map, © Merrill C. Oaks.
48 Narrow strip of wilderness, © Merrill C. Oaks.
48 Chamula indians, © Merrill C. Oaks.
48 Grijalva River, © Phil Skousen.
50 Grijalva Valley, © Merrill C. Oaks.
50 Ruins of Palenque, © Merrill C. Oaks.
51 Chiapa de Corzo ruins, © Merrill C. Oaks.
53 Guatemalan women displaying produce, © Merrill C. Oaks.
53 Weights, © Merrill C. Oaks.
54 Pyramid at Tikal, © Merrill C. Oaks.
56 Jaguar, © photo stock.
57 Pyramid in the Petén, by Mark Peterson.
57 Ruins at Laman Ayin, by Mark Peterson.
58 Becán earthworks, by Mark Peterson.
59 Crocodile, © Phil Skousen.
60 Banana tree flower, © Phil Skousen.
60 Jungle canopy above Tikal, © Robert Hawkes.
60 Red flower, © Phil Skousen.
61 Jade necklace, photography by Leon Woodward.
62 Native vegetation, © Phil Skousen.
64 Grove at Dzibanche, by Blake Allen.
65 Ruins at Dzibanche (all), by Mark Peterson.
66 Girl among ruins at Becán, by Mark Peterson.
67 Girl among ruins at Becán, by Mark Peterson.
68 Relief sculpture showing Quetzal feathered headdress figure, by Mark Peterson.
69 Relief sculpture in Chetumal, by Mark Peterson.
70 Olmec monument, © Phil Skousen.
73 Olmec heads (all), © Phil Skousen.
73 Mosaic, © Phil Skousen.
74 Lake Catemaco, © Phil Skousen.
75 Olmec figure with corn headdress, photography by Leon Woodward.
76 View from the top of Hill Vigia, © Phil Skousen.
76 Hill Cin, © David Asay.
78 Stone monument at La Venta, © Phil Skousen.
79 Defaced Olmec monument, © David Asay.
79 Serpent motif, © Cliff Dunstan.
80 Fruit stand, © Phil Skousen.
80 Pyramid in La Venta, © Merrill C. Oaks.
81 Drawing of Monument #47 at San Lorenzo, © Cliff Dunstan.
82 Ruins of Monte Albán, © Merrill C. Oaks.
82 Spear head, photography by Leon Woodward.
84 Jade dancer, photography by Leon Woodward.
85 Building over old ruins at Monte Albán, © Merrill C. Oaks.
85 (bottom left) Glyphs on stones at Monte Albán, © David Asay.
85 (bottom center) Ruins of Monte Albán, © Merrill C. Oaks.
85 Detail of architecture at Mitla, © Merrill C. Oaks.
86 Jade figure carrying load on head, photography by Leon Woodward.
87 Woman making pottery, © Merrill C. Oaks.
87 Model of Monte Albán, © Merrill C. Oaks.
88 Pyramid of the Sun at Teotihuacan, © Phil Skousen.
90 Obsidian figurine, photography by Leon Woodward.
91 Temple of Quetzalcoatl, © Merrill C. Oaks.
91 Avenue of the Dead in Teotihuacan, © Phil Skousen.
91 Looking up at the Pyramid of the Sun, © Phil Skousen.
91 Pyramid of the Sun, Teotihuacan, © Phil Skousen.
92 Drawings of Stela 31 at Tikal, Guatemala, © Cliff Dunstan.
94 *Well of Bolonchen,* by Frederick Catherwood, *Views of Ancient Monuments in Central America, Chiapas and Yucatan,* 1844, London: Archivio White Star.
97 Drawing of the hierarchy of the Mayans, © Cliff Dunstan.
97 *Ornament over Principal Doorway Casa del Covernador Uxmal,* by Frederick Catherwood, *Views of Ancient Monuments in Central America, Chiapas and Yucatan,* 1844, London: Archivio White Star.
98 Jade and obsidian knife, photography by Leon Woodward.
100 Guatemala City Temple, © Merrill C. Oaks.
102 Guatemalan woman and child, © Phil Skousen.
102 Villahermosa Temple, © Phil Skousen.
102 Mexico City Temple, © Phil Skousen.
105 Mural of Benito Juarez, © Merrill C. Oaks.

| 2500 BC | 2000 BC | 1500 BC | 1000 BC |

SAN JOSE MAGOTÉ, OAXACA
(OLMEC) 2600 BC–600 BC

SAN LORENZO, VERACRUZ
(OLMEC) 1500 BC–300 BC

LA VENTA, TABASCO
(OLMEC) 1500 BC–300 BC

TRES ZAPOTES, VERACRUZ
(OLMEC) 1500 BC–300 BC

IZAPA, CHIAPAS, MEXICO
(OLMEC/MAYA) 1200 BC–AD 1200

KAMINALJUYU, GUATEMALA
(OLMEC/MAYA) 1200 BC–AD 1200

The Mulekites (or people of Zarahemla) were part of all three civilizations mentioned in the Book of Mormon: Jaredites from 500–200 B.C.; Nephites from 200 B.C.–A.D. 350; and Lamanites from A.D. 350–900.

JAREDITES

- OLMEC
- OLMEC/MAYA
- MAYA
- ZAPOTEC
- TEOTIHUACAN
- TOLTEC
- AZTEC